John Hunt

From Adam to Webern:

The Recordings of von Karajan

Travis & Emery Music Bookshop

From Adam to Webern:
The Recordings of von Karajan

First published, John Hunt [1987].

Republished Travis & Emery 2009.

Published by
Travis & Emery Music Bookshop
17 Cecil Court, London, WC2N 4EZ, United Kingdom.
(+44) 20 7240 2129
neworders@travis-and-emery.com

ISBN Hardback: 978-1-906857-13-4   Paperback: 978-1-906857-14-1

Publisher's Foreword

Having compiled two discographies of Wilhelm Furtwängler, I became encouraged to undertake a similar venture on another great conducting figure who has been of special significance to my musical experience. In addition, when the opportunity arose to combine this with a collaboration with Stephen Pettitt on presenting the discography of the Philharmonia Orchestra, I was more than delighted. For it is this British orchestra without doubt that has been involved in so many of the great evenings I have enjoyed over a period of thirty years of concert-going and listening to records.

The idea of combining two discographies in one volume was also attractive economically, yet it is hoped that record collectors who acquire it because of their interest in one of the parts may also increase their knowledge of the other. Not that the connection between Karajan and the Philharmonia is tenuous: it was this conductor, at the outset of his post-war career, who exercised such a formative influence on the Philharmonia, which its founder Walter Legge always intended should most closely resemble in style and character its great continental counterparts in Berlin and Vienna.

Our brief in both parts has been to provide a practical guide for the average record collector. The Karajan discography is arranged by composer, which is of special interest, I think, for a conducting figure who has been so prolific and who has returned many times to re-record important works in the standard repertoire. On the other hand, the Philharmonia discography is arranged chronologically, enabling the reader to get some idea of the orchestra's development since its foundation forty-two years ago.

Both parts are arranged in three columns which we have tried to render easy on the eye. The centre column lists all artists participating in a recording, and the third one contains the catalogue numbers of the various issues. These numbers are the British rather than the continental or USA ones, the guiding pattern being a record's first issue number (and any subsequent LP issue of a 78 rpm original), important re-issues (often in less expensive editions) and the most recent incarnations including, where applicable, the Compact Disc version, <u>which is indicated by being underlined.</u> Overseas numbers are included for certain re-issues or where an item was never published in UK. EPs (extended play 7" microgroove discs) which were popular for the first decade or more of the LP era, have been ignored, except in cases where they constituted the only issue of a title.

Single LPs devoted to selections from major works are included, but not, with important exceptions, compilations including recordings of conductors and orchestras other than Karajan and the Philharmonia respectively (an asterisk against the catalogue number indicates that a work is contained in a multiple-LP edition devoted to the same artists). For the first twenty years of LP, both Deutsche Grammophon and Electrola on the continent tended to re-package and re-issue much more frequently, particularly in the case of compilations of shorter works, but on the whole these have been ignored as being of less importance in the history of a particular recording.

Operatic arias and other vocal excerpts are given in the language in which they are sung, but it is realised that in the case of many early issues where the discs have not been sighted or heard by

Contents

the compilers, consistency on this point has not been possible. Nor have original language titles been attempted in the case of Russian and Czech opera.

Although we are concerned with gramophone recordings, made in the objective atmosphere of the studio (except, that is, for the live recordings included which have been published on LP or CD), care has been taken to present the information in the light of the artists' concert activities, and to capture some of the changing style in advertising by reproducing publicity material used at the time of issue.

In almost all cases, the term "live recording" implies concert or opera performances taped illicitly in the theatre or off the air and then published unofficially without the sanction of the participating artists. A tendency in the 1980's has been for Deutsche Grammophon to publish certain recordings which have been assembled from actual performance but nonetheless recorded to the highest professional standard. Our term "live recording" has therefore not been applied to such recordings.

In conclusion, I have to state that my task of compiling and editing would have been impossible without the assistance of a number of friends and collectors who have patiently helped me to fill in gaps and to make the two discographies as comprehensive as possible within the given terms of reference. I therefore thank Paul Bowen, Clifford Elkin and David Lampon; Dr Elisabeth Legge-Schwarzkopf; Bill Holland and Alfred Kaine, both of Deutsche Grammophon; and Malcolm Granger of EMI Records.

John Hunt

The Recordings of Herbert von Karajan

Page	Section
6	Introduction
12	Discography
124	Index of artists (Appendix A)
131	Video recordings (Appendix B)
134	A personal top twenty-five (Appendix C)

Philharmonia Discography

Page	Section
142	Introduction
147	1945
149	1946
159	1947
171	1948
180	1949-1951
211	1952-1953
251	1954-1963
391	1964-1971
437	1972-1976
461	1977-1987
511	Philharmonia conductors (Appendix A)
516	Index of works (Appendix B)
535	Recording venues (Appendix C)

The Recordings of Herbert von Karajan
John Hunt;
Philharmonia Discography
Stephen J. Pettitt
edited by John Hunt

Published and copyright 1987 by John Hunt

Designed by
Richard Chlupaty, London
Printed by
Short Run Press, Exeter

ISBN 0 9510268 1 X
Further copies obtainable from John Hunt, Flat 6, 37 Chester Way, London SE11 4UR

Photograph: Siegfried Lauterwasser

1

John Hunt

From Adam to Webern: the recordings of Herbert von Karajan

To Nicky
Faithful friend
February 1972-December 1986

1987

Introduction

Herbert von Karajan takes his recording activities, and their implication for future listeners, probably more seriously than any other classical recording artist in our commercially minded age. What has become clear to me in the course of preparing this survey is the remarkable degree of organisation and planning in a 50 year recording career thats puts most other much-recorded artists to shame.

I would divide Karajan's recording career into four distinct but overlapping phases :-
1. The 78s - 1938-1942, mainly in Berlin but also sessions in Amsterdam and Turin (Polydor series), and 1946-1950, post-war Vienna (Columbia LX series).
2. The Philharmonia period 1948-1960, Columbia LPs (preceded by some 78s) with the prefix 33CX and later stereo equivalent SAX series.
3. The first Berlin period 1957-1976 (a few Columbias but mainly for Deutsche Grammophon) plus recordings in Berlin for EMI (ASD, SLS series) and in Vienna for Decca (LXT/SXL series).
4. Starting 1975-6 with the second complete Beethoven symphony cycle for DG in Berlin, where the emphasis is now firmly placed, but still with occasional sessions for EMI, Decca and Philips.

At each stage of technical innovation and improvement, Karajan has been in the forefront (LP, stereo, quadrophonic, Laservision, digital, CD). In the last decade many performances have been filmed, and we look forward in the not too distant future to these becoming commercially available on Laserdisc (many such recordings are already in circulation in Japan, and an appendix of the existing material can be found at the end of this discography).

It is probably in the third of the above periods, both in the recording studio and in the concert hall, that Karajan's performances have aroused most controversy or have failed to meet universal approval, and I quote this brief extract from a British record magazine from the mid 1970s as an indication of a certain prevalent attitude towards the work of Herbert von Karajan :

"The playing is stunningly beautiful and the readings bear all the hallmarks of Karajan's remarkable instinct for musical organisation, his ability to take a 'consensus' view of a familiar classic and dress it up in the most glamorous fashion with a master-couturier's skill. The results are both streamlined and glamorous, but almost totally predictable because the performances reveal no underlying motivation."

Karajan's own contention is that every piece of music should emerge as a thing of beauty, be it by Bach, Brahms or Webern, and that failure to prepare the piece for the most perfect realisation possible is tantamount to sitting down to a good meal without washing one's hands. He has even, on occasion, asked doubting critics if they would feel happier if the musical performance were to include a few wrong notes or false entries ! Unfortunately, a generalised version of these critical reservations has tended to become applied to most of the DG studio work of the 1960s. Now can we really dismiss a period of Karajan's work which produced gramophone classics like Debussy's "La Mer", the last four Sibelius Symphonies and an integral version of Wagner's "Ring" quite unlike any other attempted for the gramophone, not to mention astounding performances of Shostakovich's Tenth or Prokofiev's Fifth Symphonies ?

Over the years certain soloists have been engaged to work with Karajan but have failed to respond to his direction, complaining of a lack of communication (Claudio Arrau tells of such an experience when performing with Karajan and the Philharmonia at an Edinburgh Festival in the 1950s; much more recently a projected recording of the Tchaikovsky Piano Concerto with Pogorelich and Karajan came to grief, although this incident may tell us more about the younger man's inability to face reality). To my ears Karajan in fact leaves his partners a degree of freedom and imagination which only the most confident soloist, with a strong but flexible view of his own conception of the piece, will respond to. And even artists possessing the egos of the Italian tenors Mario del Monaco and Franco Corelli can be heard in recordings to have worked with the conductor in the most harmonious way, yet retaining their own individual temperament.

A similar willingness to respond is demanded of the listener to Karajan's recordings, an openness which the critic quoted above singularly fails to display. It is my view that the only thing lacking in Karajan's performances from the 1960s, or from any other period, is any gimmickry or point-making; and it is the same lack of effect-seeking - other than that prescribed by the composer's instructions - that seems to infuriate critics of Karajan in his Salzburg role of opera producer

It is these opera performances above all that are indelibly imprinted on the memories of regular Salzburg visitors (since 1957, when Karajan began his permanent association with the Salzburg Festival, I have heard all the stage works which he has directed there), but not far behind them follow the series of great choral masterpieces, marvellously integrated in Karajan's hands (Bach, Haydn, Mozart, Beethoven, Brahms, Verdi, Bruckner) and, last but not least, the symphonic repertoire. In the concert hall, as in the recording studio, Karajan has honed his conception of a work like Beethoven No 8 from early on (Walter Legge, in "On and Off the Record" tells of the endless searching for balances and textures in one of the very first post-war sessions in Vienna) to the potent and vibrant fullness of his latest, mid-80s, version of the symphony, of which an American reviewer has written :

"In his long, distinguished leadership of the Berlin Philharmonic, Karajan has honed the group into an incredibly smooth, utterly responsive performing ensemble, raising it from an already thoroughly respected status among European orchestras to one of world's greatest. What is especially praiseworthy about this performance is that, far from resting on his laurels, Karajan seems to have found new aspects of a much-played work to explore. Special care seems to have been taken with voicings, for example, so that details that often fly by in the first movement are clearly heard and add to the superb logic of the performance....there is a sensitivity to the signaling of harmonic changes that seems more highly developed than in past Karajan traversals. (By signaling, I mean the subtle indication that something is about to happen, immediately before it actually takes place)"

For an understanding of Karajan's unquestionable consistency as a conductor of his countryman Bruckner I would refer the reader to the reviews of Karajan's Bruckner recordings by Richard Osborne which have appeared in the last few years in the pages of "Gramophone". But what about Karajan's performances of his other countrymen, Haydn, Mozart and Schubert ? An acquaintance of mine who finds the cult of beauty entirely unsympathetic once described a set of Mozart Symphonies recorded for EMI in the early 70s as quite "obscene" in their richness. I could see what he meant, and they cannot be to the taste of those who prefer their Mozart played on period instruments. But if you enjoy these masterpieces viewed as the early manifestations of the 19th century symphony - and if your ear can adjust, in those particular recordings, to the slightly over-reverberant acoustic, there is reward enough in the listening.

A singer who worked extensively under Karajan's baton both in the theatre and recording studios told me recently that she had expected that the maestro, with his striving for beauty and his own personal vanity (yes, he has this and other human weaknesses !), would withdraw from public performance as his health and mobility declined, and indulge his obsession with technical matters. But on the contrary, physical frailty has added a dimension of nobility and warmth to the concerts which Karajan continues to give as he enters his eightieth year. Certainly on the evidence of his London concert in June 1987, with two Brahms symphonies, the new cycle of Brahms recordings, understood to have been completed but not yet published, should offer stiff but complementary competition to his two earlier Berlin cycles and the even earlier versions of separate Brahms symphonies with the Vienna Philharmonic and Philharmonia Orchestras.

Almost twenty years ago, Karajan's Austrian biographer Ernst Häussermann included in a discography a war-time 78 disc of Donizetti's "Don Pasquale" Overture by Karajan and the Dresden Philharmonic Orchestra. I asked Anthony Williams why he did not include this in his Karajan discography published in 1978 by General Gramophone Publications, to which Mr Williams replied:- "Karajan never conducted the Dresden Philharmonic on record to my knowledge ('Dresden Philharmonic' was, I think, a pseudonym in any case). The recording to which you refer on Cetra OR 5029 was conducted by Van Kempen."

Readers will note the inclusion of the EMI Toshiba catalogue numbers EAC 37001-19 and EAC 37020-38, which was a two-volume issue comprising, despite its numbering, 40 LPs and devoted to Karajan's entire mono recordings with the Philharmonia Orchestra, excluding the complete opera recordings. Published around 1980 in Japan and by now possibly out of print, it was this edition which filled the remaining gaps in my own collection and, indirectly, inspired me to undertake the discography.

This Karajan discography aims to list all the commercially made gramophone recordings over almost fifty years, both published and unpublished, together with unofficial live recordings issued more recently in LP and CD form. The latter do not, it must be emphasised, have the approval of the conductor - indeed, were produced illicitly and in some cases are technically inadequate. Nonetheless, they round out the picture of works in the Karajan repertoire, illustrating in certain cases an amazing consistency with officially recorded versions, and in others showing certain characteristics not always present in the studio recordings. They also provide a tantalising glimpse of Karajan at work in operas which he has not recorded commercially: "Lucia di Lammermoor", "La Traviata", "Tannhäuser". While on the subject of pirate recordings, I must make it clear that although I am involved in record retailing, I am in no way connected with the Italian organisation producing pirate CDs which has adopted the name of "Hunt Productions".

Much has been written about Herbert von Karajan, but to my mind none of the volumes devoted to his life and career do justice to this enigmatic figure, allowing his human foibles to blur the assessment of his work. Might my own modest tribute, in the form of a factual discography, say perhaps more about the essentials of Karajan's achievement than the effusiveness of both journalists and embittered acolytes ?

John Hunt

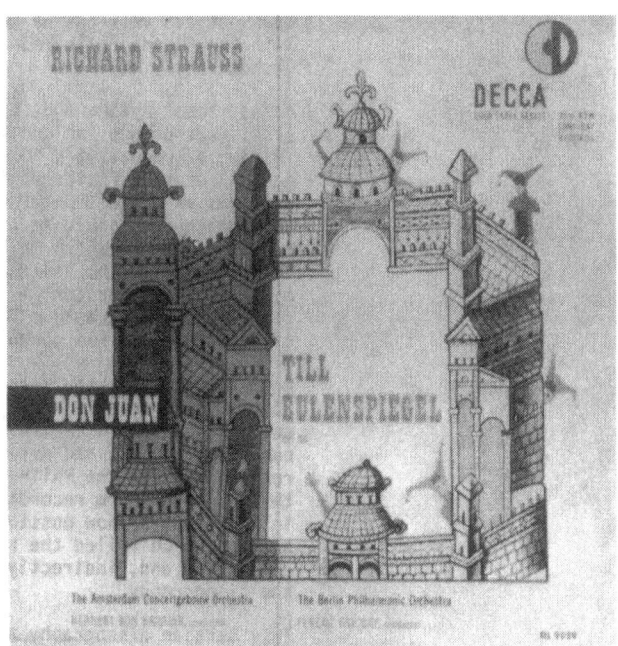

Adam

Giselle (original abridged version)

Vienna September 1961	VPO	Decca LXT 6002/SXL 6002
		Decca JB 14
		Decca 417 738-2

O Holy Night (arr. Totzauer)

Vienna June 1961	VPO	Decca LXT 5657/SXL 2294
		Decca JB 38

Albinoni

Adagio (arr. Giazotto)

St Moritz August 1969	BPO	DG 2530 247
	Schwalbé	DG 415 201-1
		DG 419 046-1
		DG 415 301-2
		DG 419 488-1
		DG 419 046-2
Berlin September 1983	BPO	DG 413 309-1
	Spierer	DG 413 309-2

Bach

Brandenburg Concertos Nos 1, 2 and 3

St Moritz August 1954	BPO	DG LPM 18 976/7/8*
		DG SLPM 138 976/7/8*
		DG LPM 39 005/SLPM 139 005
		DG 2709 016*
		DG 2725 080*
		DG 2535 488
		DG 413 185-1*
Berlin July 1978 and January 1979	BPO	DG 2707 112*
		DG 2531 332
		DG 415 374-2*

Brandenburg Concertos Nos 4, 5 and 6

St Moritz August 1954	BPO	DG LPM 18 976/7/8*
		DG SLPM 138 976/7/8*
		DG LPM 39 006/SLPM 139 006
		DG 2709 016*
		DG 2726 080*
		DG 2535 489
		DG 413 185-1*
Berlin July 1978 and January 1979	BPO	DG 2707 112*
		DG 2531 333
		DG 415 374-2*

Orchestral Suites Nos 2 and 3

St Moritz August 1964   BPO   DG LPM 18 976/7/8*
                         Zöller   DG SLPM 138 976/7/8*
                                                      DG LPM 39 007/SLPM 139 007
                                                      DG 2709 016*
                                                      DG 2535 138

Air (Orchestral Suite No 3)

Berlin September 1983   BPO   DG 413 309-1
                                                      DG 413 309-2

Magnificat in D

Berlin December 1977   BPO   DG 2531 048
                         Choir of Deutsche Oper   DG 2531 342
                         Tomowa-Sintow, Baltsa,
                         Schreier, Luxon

Mass in B minor

Vienna November 1952   Philharmonia (arias)   Columbia 33CX 1121/2/3
(choruses) and London   Vienna Singverein and   World Records T 854/5/6
November 1952 and   Orchestra (choruses)   EMI RLS 746
July 1953 (arias)   Schwarzkopf, Höffgen,   EMI 29 09743
                         Gedda, Rehfuss

Salzburg August 1962   VPO   Movimento Musica 03.012
(Live)   Vienna Singverein
                         Price, C.Ludwig,
                         Gedda, Souzay, Berry

Berlin September 1973   BPO   DG 2740 112
                         Vienna Singverein   DG 415 022-1
                         Janowitz, C.Ludwig, Kerns,
                         Schreier, Ridderbusch

Saint Matthew Passion

Vienna June 1950   Vienna Symphony   Foyer FO 1046
(Live)   Vienna Singverein
                         Seefried, Ferrier, Sterba,
                         Felbermayer, Rathauscher,
                         Stowasser, W.Ludwig, Berry,
                         Edelmann, Schöffler, Uhl,
                         Kaufmann, Pröglhöf, Wiener

Berlin December 1971,   BPO   DG 2720 070
January, February, June, Vienna Singverein   DG 419 789-2
July and November 1972   Janowitz, C.Ludwig,
                         Schreier, Laubenthal,
                         Fischer-Dieskau,
                         Berry, Diakov

Vom Himmel hoch (arr. Meyer)

Vienna June 1961	VPO Vienna Singverein Price	Decca LXT 5657/SXL 2294 Decca JB 38

Ave Maria (arr. Gounod/Sabatini)

Vienna June 1961	VPO Price	Decca LXT 5657/SXL 2294 Decca JB 38

Balakirev

Symphony No 1

London November 1949	Philharmonia	Columbia LX 1323/4/5/6/7/8 (Auto LX 8746/7/8/9/50/51) Columbia 33CX 1002 Toshiba EAC 37020-38* EMI XLP 60001 EMI RLS 7715*

Bartók

Concerto for Orchestra

London December 1951, November 1952 and July 1953	Philharmonia	Columbia 33CX 1054 Toshiba EAC 37020-38*
Berlin September and November 1965	BPO	DG LPM 39 003/SLPM 139 003 DG 2535 202 DG 415 322-2
Berlin May 1974	BPO	EMI ASD 3046

Music for Strings, Percussion and Celesta

London November 1949	Philharmonia	Columbia LX 1371/2/3/4 (Auto LX 8781/2/3/4) American Columbia ML 4456 Toshiba EAC 37020-38*
Berlin November 1960	BPO	Columbia 33CX 1783 Columbia SAX 2432 EMI SXLP 30536 EMI 1C 137 54350/1/2/3*
Berlin September 1969	BPO	DG 2530 065 DG 2542 134 DG 415 322-2

Beethoven

Symphony No 1

London November 1953	Philharmonia	Columbia 33CX 1136 World Records SM 143-149* EMI SLS 5053* Toshiba EAC 37001-19*
Berlin December 1961	BPO	DG KL 1-8/SKL 101-8* DG LPM 18 801/SLPM 138 801 DG 2720 007* DG 2721 055* DG 2542 102
Berlin January 1975	BPO	DG 2740 172/2721 200* DG 2531 101 DG 419 048-1 DG 419 048-2
Berlin January 1984	BPO	DG 415 505-1 DG 415 505-2 DG 415 066-1* DG 415 066-2*

Symphony No 2

London November 1953	Philharmonia	Columbia 33CX 1227 World Records SM 143-149* EMI SLS 5053* Toshiba EAC 37001-19*
Berlin December 1961	BPO	DG KL 1-8/SKL 101-8* DG LPM 18 801/SLPM 138 801 DG 2720 007* DG 2721 055* DG 2542 102
Berlin March 1977	BPO	DG 2740 172/2721 200* DG 2531 101 DG 419 050-1 DG 419 050-2
Berlin February 1984	BPO	DG 415 505-1 DG 415 505-2 DG 415 066-1* DG 415 066-2*

Symphony No 3 "Eroica"

London November and December 1952	Philharmonia	Columbia 33CX 1046 World Records SM 143-149* EMI SLS 5053* Toshiba EAC 37001-19*
Berlin September 1953 (Live)	BPO	Maestri del Secolo APE 1205 WG Records WG 30003
Berlin November 1962	BPO	DG KL 1-8/SKL 101-8* DG LPM 18 802/SLPM 138 802 DG 2720 007* DG 2721 055* DG 2542 103
Berlin May 1976	BPO	DG 2740 172/2721 200* DG 2531 103 DG 419 049-1 DG 419 049-2
Berlin January 1984	BPO	DG 415 506-1 DG 415 506-2 DG 415 066-1* DG 415 066-1*

Symphony No 4

London November 1953	Philharmonia	Columbia 33CX 1278 World Records SM 143-149* EMI SLS 5053* Toshiba EAC 37001-19*
Berlin November 1962	BPO	DG KL 1-8/SKL 101-8* DG LPM 18 803/SLPM 138 803 DG 2720 007* DG 2721 055* DG 2542 104
Berlin September 1976	BPO	DG 2740 172/2721 200* DG 2531 104 DG 419 048-1 DG 419 048-2
Berlin December 1983	BPO	DG 415 121-1 DG 415 121-2 DG 415 066-1* DG 415 066-2*

Symphony No 5

Vienna November 1948	VPO	Columbia LX 1330/1/2/3 (Auto LX 8752/3/4/5) Columbia 33CX 1004 Toshiba EAC 30111
London August 1953	Philharmonia	Columbia unpublished
London November 1954	Philharmonia	Columbia 33CX 1266 World Records SM 143-149* EMI SLS 5053* Toshiba EAC 37001-19*
Berlin February 1962	BPO	DG KL 1-8/SKL 101-8* DG LPM 18 804/SLPM 138 804 DG 2720 007* DG 2721 055* DG 2542 105
Berlin October 1976	BPO	DG 2740 172/2721 200* DG 2531 105 DG 419 051-1 DG 419 051-2
Berlin November 1982	BPO	DG 413 933-1 DG 413 932-2 DG 415 066-1* DG 415 066-2*

Symphony No 6 "Pastoral"

London July 1953	Philharmonia	Columbia 33CX 1124 World Records SM 143-149* EMI SLS 5053* Toshiba EAC 37001-19*
Berlin February 1962	BPO	DG KL 1-8/SKL 101-8* DG LPM 18 805/SLPM 138 805 DG 2720 007* DG 2721 055* DG 2542 106
Berlin October 1976	BPO	DG 2740 172/2721 200* DG 2531 106 DG 415 833-1 DG 415 833-2
Berlin November 1982	BPO	DG 413 936-1 DG 413 932-2 DG 415 066-1* DG 415 066-2*

Symphony No 7

Berlin 1941	Berlin Staatskapelle	Polydor 67643/4/5/6/7/8
London November 1951 and April and May 1952	Philharmonia	Columbia 33CX 1035 World Records SM 143-149* EMI SLS 5053* Toshiba EAC 37001-19*
Vienna March 1959	VPO	RCA RB 16212/SB 2087 Decca SDD 232
Berlin March 1962	BPO	DG KL 1-8/SKL 101-8* DG LPM 18 806/SLPM 138 806 DG 2720 007* DG 2721 055* DG 2542 107
Berlin October 1976	BPO	DG 2740 172/2721 200* DG 2531 107 DG 419 050-1 DG 419 050-2
Berlin December 1983	BPO	DG 415 121-1 DG 415 121-2 DG 415 066-1* DG 415 066-2*

Symphony No 8

Vienna September 1946	VPO	Columbia LX 988/89/90 (Auto LX 8557/8/9) Toshiba EAC 30102 EMI RLS 7714*
London May 1955 (previous sessions in November 1953)	Philharmonia	Mono version Columbia 33CX 1391/2* Toshiba EAC 37001-19* Stereo version World Records SM 143-149* EMI SLS 5053* Toshiba EAC 37001-19*
Berlin January 1962	BPO	DG KL 1-8/SKL 101-8* DG LPM 18 807-8/SLPM 138 807-8* DG 139 015 DG 2720 007* DG 2721 055* DG 2725 101*
Berlin October 1976	BPO	DG 2740 172/2721 200* DG 2707 109* DG 419 051-1 DG 419 051-2
Berlin February 1984	BPO	DG 415 507-1 DG 415 507-2 DG 415 066-1* DG 415 066-2*

Symphony No 9 "Choral"

Vienna November and December 1947 and	VPO Vienna Singverein Schwarzkopf, Höngen, Patzak, Hotter	Columbia LX 1097/8/9/1100/1/ 2/3/4/5 (Auto LX 8612/3/4/5/6/7/8/9/ 8620) Toshiba EAC 30101 EMI RLS 7714*
Vienna July 1955	Philharmonia Vienna Singverein Schwarzkopf, Höffgen, Häfliger, Edelmann	Columbia 33CX 1391/2 World Records SM 143-149* EMI SLS 5053* Toshiba EAC 37001-19*
Berlin April 1957 (Live)	BPO St.Hedwig's Cathedral Choir Grümmer, Höffgen, Häfliger, Frick	Maestri del Secolo APE 1209 Movimento Musica 08.001* Replica SRPL 22400 WG Records WG 30009
Berlin October 1962	BPO Vienna Singverein Janowitz, Rössl-Majdan, Kmennt, Berry	DG KL 1-8/SKL 101-8* DG LPM 18 807-8/SLPM 138 807-8 DG 2720 007* DG 2721 055* DG 2725 101 Rehearsal extract: DG 643 201
Berlin September 1976	BPO Vienna Singverein Tomowa-Sintow, Baltsa, Schreier, Van Dam	DG 2740 172/2721 200* DG 2707 109 DG 415 832-1 DG 415 832-2
Berlin September 1983	BPO Vienna Singverein Perry, Baltsa, Cole, Van Dam	DG 413 933-1 DG 410 987-2 DG 415 066-1* DG 415 066-2*

The European Anthem (arr. Karajan)

Berlin February and March 1972	BPO	DG 2530 250

York March (arr. Schade)

Berlin March 1973	BPO Wind & Brass Ensemble	DG 2721 077* DG 2535 647 DG 2535 686

Grosse Fuge in B flat

St Moritz August 1969	BPO	DG 2530 066

Piano Concerto No 1

Berlin November 1966	BPO Eschenbach	DG 139 023 DG 2535 273 DG 410 837-1
Berlin September 1977	BPO Weissenberg	EMI SLS 5112*

Piano Concerto No 2

Berlin September 1977	BPO Weissenberg	EMI SLS 5112*

Piano Concerto No 3

Berlin September 1977	BPO Weissenberg	EMI SLS 5112*

Piano Concerto No 4

London June 1951	Philharmonia Gieseking	Columbia LX 1443/4/5/6 (Auto LX 8831/2/3/4) Columbia 33C 1007 EMI 3C 153 52425-31M* Toshiba EAC 37001-19*
Berlin September 1976	BPO Weissenberg	EMI SLS 5112*

Piano Concerto No 5 "Emperor"

London June 1951	Philharmonia Gieseking	International Columbia LCX 5008/9/10/11/12 Columbia 33CX 1010 EMI 3C 153 52425-31M* Toshiba EAC 37001-19*
Berlin September 1974	BPO Weissenberg	EMI ASD 3043 EMI SLS 5112*

Violin Concerto

Berlin January 1967	BPO Ferras	DG 139 021 DG 2740 137* DG 419 052-1
Berlin September 1979	BPO Mutter	DG 2531 250 DG 413 818-2

Triple Concerto

Berlin September 1969	BPO Richter, Oistrakh, Rostropovich	EMI ASD 2582
Berlin September 1979	BPO Zeltser, Mutter, Ma	DG 2531 262 DG 415 276-2

Missa Solemnis

Vienna September 1958	Philharmonia Vienna Singverein Schwarzkopf, C.Ludwig, Gedda, Zaccaria	Columbia 33CX 1634/5 World Records ST 914/5 EMI SLS 5198
Salzburg August 1959 (Live)	VPO Vienna Singverein Price, C.Ludwig, Gedda, Zaccaria	Melodram MEL 704
Berlin February 1966	BPO Vienna Singverein Janowitz, C.Ludwig, Wunderlich, Berry	DG KL 95-6/SKL 195-6 DG 2707 030 DG 2721 135/2720 013* DG 2726 048
Berlin September 1974	BPO Vienna Singverein Janowitz, Baltsa, Schreier, Van Dam	EMI SLS 979 EMI CFP 41 4420-3
Berlin September 1985	BPO Vienna Singverein Cuberli, T.Schmidt, Cole, Van Dam	DG 419 166-1 DG 419 166-2

Ah Perfido, Concert aria

Watford September 1954	Philharmonia Schwarzkopf	Columbia 33CX 1278 Toshiba EAC 37001-19* EMI RLS 7715*

Consecration of the House, Overture

London July 1954	Philharmonia	Columbia unpublished (recording incomplete)
Berlin January 1969	BPO	DG 2721 137/2720 011* DG 2707 046* DG 2726 079*

Coriolan, Overture

London June and July 1953	Philharmonia	Columbia 33CX 1227 EMI SLS 5053* Toshiba EAC 37001-19*
Berlin September 1965	BPO	DG 139 001 DG 139 015 DG 2721 137/2720 011* DG 2707 046* DG 2530 414 DG 2726 079* DG 2542 141 DG 410 837-1 DG 415 276-2 DG 415 833-1 DG 415 833-2
Berlin December 1985	BPO	DG 415 507-1 DG 415 507-2 DG 415 066-1* DG 415 066-2*

Egmont, Incidental Music to Goethe's drama

Berlin January 1969	BPO Janowitz, Schellow	DG 2721 137/2720 011* DG 2530 301 DG 419 624-2

Egmont, Overture

London June and July 1953	Philharmonia	Columbia 33CX 1136 EMI SLS 5053* Toshiba EAC 37001-19*
Berlin January 1969	BPO	DG 2721 137/2720 011* DG 2707 046* DG 2530 414 DG 2726 079* DG 2542 141 DG 415 276-2 DG 419 048-1 DG 419 048-2
Berlin December 1985	BPO	DG 415 506-1 DG 415 506-2 DG 415 066-1* DG 415 066-2*

Fidelio

Salzburg July 1957 (Live)	VPO Vienna State Opera Chorus Goltz, Jurinac, Zampieri, Kmennt, Majkut, Schöffler, Edelmann, Zaccaria, Berry	Melodram MEL 040
Milan December 1960 (Live)	La Scala Orchestra and Chorus Nilsson, Lipp, Vickers, Unger, Gullino, Mantovani, Hotter, Frick, Crass,	HRE Records HRE 388
Vienna May 1962 (Live)	VPO Vienna State Opera Chorus C. Ludwig, Janowitz, Vickers, Kmennt, Kreppel, Berry, Wächter, Paskalis, Pantscheff	Movimento Musica 03.014
Berlin October and December 1970	BPO Chorus of Deutsche Oper Dernesch, Donath, Vickers, Laubenthal, Hollweg, Frese, Van Dam, Kelemen, Ridderbusch	EMI SLS 954 EMI SLS 5231 Excerpts: EMI ASD 2911

Abscheulicher, wo eilst du hin ? (Fidelio)

Watford September 1954	Philharmonia Schwarzkopf	Columbia 33CX 1266 Toshiba EAC 37001-19* EMI RLS 7715*

Fidelio, Overture

Berlin September 1965	BPO	DG 139 001 DG 139 015 DG 2721 137/2720 011* DG 2707 046* DG 2530 414 DG 2535 310 DG 2726 079* DG 2542 141 DG 415 276-2 DG 419 051-1 DG 419 051-2
Berlin December 1985	BPO	DG 415 507-1 DG 415 507-2 DG 415 066-1* DG 415 066-2*

(Additional versions of Fidelio Overture, taken from the complete opera recordings listed above, are on the following excerpt LPs: Maestri del Secolo APE 1210 and WG Records WG 30010 (Salzburg 1957), Replica SRPL 22400 (Vienna 1962) and EMI SEOM 18 and SXLP 30506 (Berlin 1970).)

King Stephen, Overture

Berlin January 1969   BPO   DG 2721 137/2720 011*
                                                        DG 2707 046*
                                                        DG 2726 079*
                                                        DG 419 052-1

Leonore No 1, Overture

Berlin January 1969   BPO   DG 2721 137/2720 011*
                                                        DG 2707 046*
                                                        DG 2726 079*

Leonore No 2, Overture

Berlin January 1969   BPO   DG 2721 137/2720 011*
                                                        DG 2707 046*
                                                        DG 2726 079*

Leonore No 3, Overture

Amsterdam 1943   Concertgebouw   Polydor 68181/2
                                                        (Auto 69182/3)

London July 1953   Philharmonia   Columbia 33CX 1136
                                                        EMI SLS 5053*
                                                        Toshiba EAC 37001-19*

Berlin September 1965   BPO   DG 139 001
                                                        DG 139 015
                                                        DG 2721 137/2720 011*
                                                        DG 2707 046*
                                                        DG 2530 414
                                                        DG 2726 079*
                                                        DG 2542 141
                                                        DG 419 049-1
                                                        DG 419 049-2

Berlin December 1985   BPO   DG 415 507-1
                                                        DG 415 507-2
                                                        DG 415 066-1*
                                                        DG 415 066-2*

(Additional versions of Leonore No 3 Overture, taken from the complete recordings
of Fidelio listed above, are on the following excerpt LPs: Maestri del Secolo
APE 1210 and WG Records WG 30010 (Salzburg 1957) and Replica SRPL 22400 (Vienna 1962).)

Namensfeier, Overture

Berlin January 1969   BPO   DG 2721 137/2720 011*
                                                        DG 2707 046*
                                                        DG 2726 079*

Prometheus, Overture

Berlin January 1969　　　　BPO　　　　　　　　DG 2721 137/2720 011*
　　　　　　　　　　　　　　　　　　　　　　　DG 2707 046*
　　　　　　　　　　　　　　　　　　　　　　　DG 2726 079*
　　　　　　　　　　　　　　　　　　　　　　　DG 419 833-1
　　　　　　　　　　　　　　　　　　　　　　　DG 419 833-2

The Ruins of Athens, Overture

Berlin January 1969　　　　BPO　　　　　　　　DG 2721 137/2720 011*
　　　　　　　　　　　　　　　　　　　　　　　DG 2707 046*
　　　　　　　　　　　　　　　　　　　　　　　DG 2530 414
　　　　　　　　　　　　　　　　　　　　　　　DG 2726 079*
　　　　　　　　　　　　　　　　　　　　　　　DG 2542 141
　　　　　　　　　　　　　　　　　　　　　　　DG 419 833-1
　　　　　　　　　　　　　　　　　　　　　　　DG 419 833-2

Wellington's Victory (Battle Symphony)

Berlin January 1969　　　　BPO　　　　　　　　DG 643 210
　　　　　　　　　　　　　　　　　　　　　　　DG 139 045
　　　　　　　　　　　　　　　　　　　　　　　DG 2538 142
　　　　　　　　　　　　　　　　　　　　　　　DG 419 624-2

Berg

Three Orchestral Pieces op 6

Berlin December 1972　　　BPO　　　　　　　　DG 2711 014*
　　　　　　　　　　　　　　　　　　　　　　　DG 2530 487
　　　　　　　　　　　　　　　　　　　　　　　DG 413 801-1

Three Pieces from Lyric Suite

Berlin December 1972　　　BPO　　　　　　　　DG 2711 014*
　　　　　　　　　　　　　　　　　　　　　　　DG 2530 487
　　　　　　　　　　　　　　　　　　　　　　　DG 413 801-1

Berlioz

Symphonie Fantastique

London July 1954　　　　　Philharmonia　　　　Columbia 33CX 1206
　　　　　　　　　　　　　　　　　　　　　　　World Records TP 625
　　　　　　　　　　　　　　　　　　　　　　　Toshiba EAC 37001-19*
　　　　　　　　　　　　　　　　　　　　　　　EMI RLS 7715*

Berlin December 1964　　　BPO　　　　　　　　DG LPM 18 964/SLPM 138 964
　　　　　　　　　　　　　　　　　　　　　　　DG 2535 256

Berlin October 1974　　　　BPO　　　　　　　　DG 2530 597
　　　　　　　　　　　　　　　　　　　　　　　DG 415 325-2

Le Carnaval Romain, Overture

London January 1958	Philharmonia	Columbia 33CX 1548 EMI SLS 5019* EMI SXLP 30450

Hungarian March (La Damnation de Faust)

London January 1958	Philharmonia	Columbia 33CX 1571 Columbia SAX 2302 EMI SLS 5019*
Berlin December 1978	BPO	EMI ASD 3761 EMI EG 29 10681

Dance of the Sylphs; Dance of the Will o' the Wisps (La Damnation de Faust)

Berlin September 1971	BPO	DG 2530 244 DG 415 856-1 DG 415 356-2

Royal Hunt and Storm (Les Troyens)

London January 1959	Philharmonia Chorus	Columbia SAX 2294 EMI SLS 5019*

Bizet

L'Arlésienne, Suite No 1

London January 1958	Philharmonia	Columbia 33CX 1608 Columbia SAX 2289 World Records ST 1044 EMI SLS 5019* EMI EMX 2028
Berlin December 1970	BPO	DG 2530 128 DG 419 469-1
Berlin September 1983 and February 1984	BPO	DG 415 106-1 DG 415 106-2

L'Arlésienne, Suite No 2

London January 1958	Philharmonia	Columbia 33CX 1608 Columbia SAX 2289 World Records ST 1044 EMI SLS 5019* (Nos. 2 & 4) EMI EMX 2028
Berlin December 1970	BPO	DG 2530 128 DG 419 469-1
Berlin December 1978	BPO	EMI ASD 3761 EMI EG 29 10681
Berlin September 1983 and February 1984	BPO	DG 415 106-1 DG 415 106-2

Carmen

Vienna October 1954 (Live)	Vienna Symphony Vienna Singverein Simionato, Güden, Sciutti, Ribacchi, Gedda, Roux, Carlin, Guthrie, Signore, Sordello,	GOP Records GFC 026/7/8
Milan December 1955 (Live)	La Scala Orchestra and Chorus Simionato, Carteri, Sciutti, Carlin, Di Stefano, Roux, Signori, Modesti, Sordello, Ribacchi	Fonit Cetra LO 22 Discocorp RR 470 Turnabout THS 65160/1/2
Vienna August 1962 and November 1963	VPO Vienna State Opera Chorus Vienna Boys Choir Price, Freni, Linval, Macaux, Corelli, Merrill, Benoit, Besancon, Demigny, Schooten	RCA LD 6164/LDS 6164 RCA SER 5600/1/2 Excerpts: RCA RB 6671/SB 6671
Berlin September 1982 (Dialogues March 1983)	BPO Chorus of Deutsche Oper Schöneberg Boys Choir Baltsa, Ricciarelli, Barbaux, Berbie, Carreras, Van Dam, Malta, Melbye, Quilico, Zednik, Tostain, Marinpouille, Pilard	DG 2741 025 DG 410 088-2 Excerpts: DG 413 322-1 DG 413 322-2

Carmen, Suite No 1

London January 1958	Philharmonia	Columbia 33CX 1608 Columbia SAX 2289 World Records ST 1044 EMI SLS 839* EMI SXDW 3048* EMI EMX 2028
Berlin December 1970	BPO	DG 2530 128 DG 413 983-1 DG 419 469-1
Berlin September 1982 (from DG version of the complete opera)	BPO	DG 415 106-1 DG 415 106-2

Carmen, Act 4 Entr'acte

London July 1954	Philharmonia	Columbia 33CX 1265 Toshiba EAC 37020-38*

Carmen, Acts 2 and 3 Entr'actes

London July 1954	Philharmonia	Columbia unpublished

Boccherini

<u>Quintettino</u>

St Moritz August 1969	BPO	DG 2530 247

Borodin

<u>Dance of the Polovtsian Maidens and Polovtsian Dances (Prince Igor)</u>

London November 1954	Philharmonia	Columbia 33CX 1327 Toshiba EAC 37020-38*
London September 1960	Philharmonia	Columbia 33CX 1774 Columbia SAX 2421 EMI SLS 5019* EMI SXDW 3048* EMI SXLP 30445 (Polovtsian Dances only)
Berlin December 1970	BPO	DG 2530 200 DG 419 063-1 <u>DG 419 063-2</u>

Brahms

<u>Symphony No 1</u>

Amsterdam 1943	Concertgebouw	Polydor 68175/6/7/8/9/70 (Auto 59176/7/8/9/80/81)
London May and July 1952	Philharmonia	Columbia 33CX 1053 Toshiba EAC 37020-38*
Washington February 1955 (Live)	BPO	Fonit Cetra LO 506* Maestri del Secolo APE 1202 WG Records WG 30001
Vienna March 1959	VPO	RCA RB 16211/SB 2086 Decca SDD 283 Decca VIV 35 <u>Decca 417 739-2</u>
Berlin November 1963	BPO	DG KL 33-39/SKL 133-139* DG LPM 18 924/SLPM 138 924 DG 2721 075/2740 242* DG 2542 166
Berlin October 1977	BPO	DG 2740 193* DG 2531 131

Symphony No 2

Vienna October and November 1949	VPO	Italian Columbia GQX 11441/2/3/4/5 French Columbia FCX 285 Angel (USA) 35007 Toshiba EAC 30106
London May 1955	Philharmonia	Columbia 33CX 1355 Toshiba EAC 37020-38* EMI SXLP 30513
Berlin November 1963	BPO	DG KL 33-39/SKL 133-139* DG LPM 18 925/SLPM 138 925 DG 2721 075/2740 242* DG 2542 167
Berlin October 1977	BPO	DG 2740 193* DG 2531 132

Symphony No 3

Vienna October 1960	VPO	Decca MET 231/SET 231 Decca SDD 284
Berlin September 1964	BPO	DG KL 33-39/SKL 133-139* DG LPM 18 926/SLPM 138 926 DG 2721 075/2740 242* DG 2542 168
Berlin October 1977	BPO	DG 2740 193* DG 2531 133

Symphony No 4

London May 1955	Philharmonia	Columbia 33CX 1362 Toshiba EAC 37020-38* EMI SXLP 30505
Berlin November 1963	BPO	DG KL 33-39/SKL 133-139* DG LPM 18 927/SLPM 138 927 DG 2721 075/2740 242* DG 2542 169
Berlin October 1977	BPO	DG 2740 193* DG 2531 134

Tragic Overture

Vienna October 1961	VPO	Decca MET 231/SET 231 Decca SDD 284 Decca 417 739-2
Berlin September and October 1970	BPO	EMI SEOM 18 EMI SLS 996* EMI SXLP 30506 EMI CFP 41 4422-3*
Berlin October 1977	BPO	DG 2740 193* DG 2531 133
Berlin February 1983	BPO	DG 410 603-1 DG 410 603-2

St Antoni Variations (Haydn Variations)

London May 1955	Philharmonia	Columbia 33CX 1349 Toshiba EAC 37001-19*
Berlin February 1964	BPO	DG KL 33-39/SKL 133-139* DG LPM 18 926/SLPM 138 926 DG 2707 018* DG 2726 078* DG 2542 168
Berlin September and October 1976	BPO	EMI SLS 996* EMI CFP 41 4422-3*

Piano Concerto No 2

Rome December 1954 (Live)	RAI Rome Orchestra Anda	Replica RPL 2467
Berlin November 1958	BPO Richter-Haaser	Columbia 33CX 1680 Columbia SAX 2328 World Records ST 1090
Berlin September 1967	BPO Anda	DG 139 034 DG 2535 263 DG 410 977-1

Violin Concerto

Berlin May 1964	BPO Ferras	DG KL 33-39/SKL 133-139* DG LPM 18 930/SLPM 138 930 DG 2740 137* DG 2542 117
Berlin March 1976	BPO Kremer	EMI ASD 3261 EMI EG 29 0274-1
Berlin September 1981	BPO Mutter	DG 2532 032 DG 400 064-2

Double Concerto

Berlin February 1983	BPO Mutter, Meneses	DG 410 603-1 DG 410 603-2

A German Requiem

Vienna October 1947	VPO Vienna Singverein Schwarzkopf, Hotter	Columbia LX 1055/6/7/8/9/ 1060/1/2/3/4 (Auto LX 8595/6/7/8/9/ 8600/1/2/3/4) Toshiba EAC 30103 EMI 2C 051 43176 EMI RLS 7714*
Berlin May 1964	BPO Vienna Singverein Janowitz, Wächter	DG KL 33-39/SKL 133-139* DG 2707 018 DG 2726 078
Berlin September and October 1976	BPO Vienna Singverein Tomowa-Sintow, Van Dam	EMI SLS 996 CFP 41 4422-3
Vienna May 1983	VPO Vienna Singverein Hendricks, Van Dam	DG 410 521-1 DG 410 521-2

Hungarian Dances Nos 1, 3, 5, 6, 17, 18, 19 and 20

Berlin September 1959	BPO	DG LPM 18 610/SLPM 138 080 DG 135 031 (Nos 1, 3, 5 and 6 only)

Britten

Frank Bridge Variations

London November 1953	Philharmonia	Columbia 33CX 1159 Toshiba EAC 37020-38* EMI XLP 60002

Bruch

Violin Concerto No 1

Berlin September 1980	BPO Mutter	DG 2532 016 DG 400 031-2

Bruckner

<u>Symphony No 1</u>

Berlin January 1981	BPO	DG 2740 264*
		DG 2532 062
		DG 415 985-2*

<u>Symphony No 2</u>

Berlin January 1981	BPO	DG 2740 264*
		DG 2532 063
		DG 415 988-2

<u>Symphony No 3</u>

Berlin September 1980	BPO	DG 2740 264*
		DG 2532 007
		DG 413 362-2

<u>Symphony No 4 "Romantic"</u>

Berlin September and October 1970	BPO	EMI SLS 811*
		EMI RLS 768*
		EMI EG 29 0566-1
		EMI CDM 769 0062
Berlin April 1975	BPO	DG 2530 674
		DG 2740 264*
		DG 415 277-2

<u>Symphony No 5</u>

Berlin December 1976	BPO	DG 2707 101
		DG 2740 264*
		DG 415 985-2

<u>Symphony No 6</u>

Berlin September 1979	BPO	DG 2531 295
		DG 2740 264*
		DG 419 194-2

<u>Symphony No 7</u>

Berlin October 1970 and February 1971	BPO	EMI SLS 811*
		EMI SLS 5086
		EMI EG 29 0858-1
Berlin April 1975	BPO	DG 2707 102
		DG 2740 264*
		DG 419 195-2

Symphony No 8

Berlin 1944 (Live performance of last movement only)	Berlin Staatskapelle	Discocorp RR 508* Discocorp RR 391*
Berlin May 1957	BPO	Columbia 33CX 1585/6 World Records ST 772/3 EMI SXDW 3024 EMI CFP 41 4434-3
Berlin January 1975	BPO	DG 2707 085 DG 2740 264* DG 419 196-2

Symphony No 9

Berlin March 1966	BPO	DG 139 011 DG 2542 129
Berlin September 1975	BPO	DG 2530 828 DG 2740 264* DG 419 083-2

Te Deum

Berlin September 1975	BPO Vienna Singverein Tomowa-Sintow, Baltsa, Schreier, Van Dam	DG 2530 704
Vienna September 1984	VPO Vienna Singverein Perry, Müller-Molinari, Winbergh, Malta	DG 410 521-1* DG 410 521-2*

Chabrier

España

Vienna December 1947	VPO	Columbia unpublished
London July 1953	Philharmonia	Columbia 33CX 1335 Toshiba EAC 37020-38*
London September 1960	Philharmonia	Columbia 33CX 1758 Columbia SAX 2404 World Records ST 838 EMI SLS 839* EMI SXDW 3048 EMI CFP 40368
Berlin December 1978	BPO	EMI ASD 3761 EMI EG 29 10681

Marche Joyeuse

London July 1955	Philharmonia	Columbia 33CX 1335 Toshiba EAC 37020-38*
London September 1960	Philharmonia	Columbia 33CX 1758 Columbia SAX 2404 World Records ST 838 EMI SLS 5019* EMI CFP 40368

Cherubini

Anacreon, Overture

Berlin 1939	Berlin Staatskapelle	Polydor 67514
Berlin January 1981	BPO	EMI ASD 4072 Toshiba CC28-99008 EMI CDM 769 0202

Chopin

Les Sylphides, Ballet Music (arr. Douglas)

Berlin April 1961	BPO	DG LPEM 19 257/SLPEM 136 257 DG 2535 189 DG 413 981-1

Cilèa

Adriana Lecouvreur, Act 2 Intermezzo

Berlin September 1967	BPO	DG 139 031 DG 419 257-2*

Corelli

Concerto Grosso op 6 no 8 "Christmas Concerto"

St Moritz August 1970	BPO	DG 2530 070 DG 2542 143 DG 415 027-1* DG 415 301-2 DG 419 046-1 DG 419 413-1 DG 419 046-2

Debussy

La Mer

London July 1953	Philharmonia	Columbia 33CX 1099 Toshiba EAC 37020-38*
Berlin March 1964	BPO	DG LPM 18 923/SLPM 138 923 DG 2542 116
Berlin January 1977	BPO	EMI ASD 3431 EMI 1C 137 54360/1/2/3* EMI EG 29 0856-1 Toshiba CC28-99007 EMI CDM 769 0072
Berlin December 1985 and February 1986	BPO	DG 413 589-1 DG 413 589-2

Prélude à l'après-midi d'un faune

Berlin March 1964	BPO	DG LPM 18 923/SLPM 138 923 DG 2542 116
Berlin January 1977	BPO	EMI ASD 3431 EMI EG 29 0856-1 Toshiba CC28-99007 EMI CDM 769 0072
Berlin December 1985 and February 1986	BPO	DG 413 589-1 DG 413 589-2

Pelléas et Melisande

Rome December 1954 (Live)	RAI Rome Orchestra and Chorus Schwarzkopf, Sciutti, Gayraud, Häfliger, Roux, Petri, Calabrese	Fonit Cetra ARK 6 Rodolphe RP 12393/4/5
Berlin December 1978	BPO Chorus of Deutsche Oper Von Stade, Barbaux, Denize, Stilwell, Van Dam, R.Raimondi, Thomas	EMI SLS 5172 EMI CDS 749 3502

Délibes

Coppélia, Ballet Suite

Berlin April 1961	BPO	DG LPEM 19 257/SLPEM 136 257 DG 2535 189 DG 413 981-1

Donizetti

Lucia di Lammermoor

Berlin September 1955 (Live)	RIAS Berlin Orchestra La Scala Chorus Callas, Villa, Di Stefano, Zampieri, Panerai, Zaccaria, Carlin	Limited Edition LER 101 BJR Records BJR 133 Morgan Records MOR 5401 Fonit Cetra LO 18 Turnabout THS 65144/5 Replica ARPL 32495 Paragon DSV 52004 Movimento Musica 02.001 Fonit Cetra ARK 5 Melodram MEL 26004 Hunt Productions HUNTCD 502 Excerpts: Rodolphe RP 12701 Movimento Musica 011.002

Lucia di Lammermoor, Act 4

Milan January 1954 (Live)	La Scala Orchestra and Chorus Di Stefano, Modesti	Melodram MEL 078* Fonit Cetra ARK 5*

Regnava nel silenzio (Lucia di Lammermoor)

Milan January 1954 (Live)	La Scala Orchestra Callas, Villa	Fonola Records ST 5010 HRE Records HRE 219*

Dvořák

Symphony No 8

Vienna October 1961	VPO	Decca LXT 6169/SXL 6169 Decca SDD 440
Berlin January 1979	BPO	EMI ASD 3775 Toshiba CC28-99003 EMI EG 29 10701
Vienna January 1985	VPO	DG 415 971-1 DG 415 971-2

Symphony No 9 "From the New World"

Berlin 1940	BPO	Polydor 67519/20/1/2/3/4
Berlin May 1958 (previous sessions in November 1957 and January 1958)	BPO	Columbia 33CX 1642 Columbia SAX 2272 EMI SLS 839* EMI ASD 2863 EMI SXLP 100 4911
Berlin March 1964	BPO	DG LPM 18 922/SLPM 138 922
Berlin January 1977	BPO	EMI ASD 3407 <u>Toshiba CC28-99002</u> <u>EMI EG 29 10701</u> <u>EMI CDM 769 0052</u>
Vienna February 1985	VPO	DG 415 509-1 <u>DG 415 509-2</u>

Cello Concerto

Berlin September 1968	BPO Rostropovich	DG 139 044 DG 2543 054 <u>DG 413 819-2</u>

Scherzo Capriccioso

Berlin September 1971	BPO	DG 2530 244 DG 2543 509

Serenade for Strings

Berlin September 1980	BPO	DG 2532 012 <u>DG 400 038-2</u>

Slavonic Dances Op 46 nos 1, 3 and 7; Op 72 nos 10 and 16

Berlin September 1959	BPO	DG LPM 18 610/SLPM 138 080 DG 2543 509

Slavonic Dance Op 46 No 8

Berlin January 1979	BPO	EMI ASD 3775 EMI SXLP 30506 <u>Toshiba CC28-99003</u>

Ertl

Hoch- und Deutschmeister March

Berlin March 1973	BPO Wind & Brass Ensemble	DG 2721 077* DG 2535 647

Franck

Symphony in D minor

Paris November 1969   Orchestre de Paris   EMI ASD 2552
                                                                                        EMI EG 29 0853-1
                                                                                        Toshiba CC28-99006
                                                                                        EMI CDM 769 0082

Symphonic Variations

London June 1951   Philharmonia   Columbia LX 8937/8
                                     Gieseking   American Columbia ML 4536
                                                               EMI 1C 047 01363M
                                                               Toshiba EAC 37001-19*

Berlin September 1972   BPO   EMI ASD 2872
                                     Weissenberg   EMI EG 29 0853-1
                                                                   Toshiba CC28-99006
                                                                   EMI CDM 769 0082

Fučík

Torgau March

Berlin March 1973   BPO Wind & Brass Ensemble   DG 2721 077*
                                                                                                DG 2535 647

Hohenfriedberg March

Berlin March 1973   BPO Wind & Brass Ensemble   DG 2721 077*

Frederick the Great

Florentine March

Berlin March 1973   BPO Wind & Brass Ensemble   DG 2721 077*
                                                                                                DG 2535 647

Children of the Regiment, March (arr. Blaha)

Berlin March 1973   BPO Wind & Brass Ensemble   DG 2721 077*

Giordano

Fedora, Act 2 Intermezzo

Berlin September 1967	BPO	DG 139 031 DG 415 856-1 DG 419 257-2* DG 415 855-2

Gluck

Orfeo ed Euridice

Salzburg August 1959 (Live)	VPO Vienna State Opera Chorus Simionato, Jurinac, Sciutti	Replica RPL 2436/7 Legendary LR 132-2

Dance of the Blessed Spirits (Orfeo ed Euridice)

Berlin September 1983	BPO	DG 413 309-1 DG 413 309-2

Gounod

Faust, Ballet Music

London January 1958	Philharmonia	Columbia 33CX 1588 Columbia SAX 2274 World Records ST 1084 EMI SLS 839* EMI SXLP 30224
Berlin January and February 1971	BPO	DG 2530 199
Berlin December 1978	BPO	EMI ASD 3761 EMI EG 29 1068l

Waltz, Faust

Berlin January and February 1971	BPO	DG 2530 199 DG 415 856-1 DG 415 855-2

Serenade: Vous qui faites l'endormie (Faust)

London November 1949	Philharmonia Christoff	HMV unpublished

Granados

<u>Goyescas, Intermezzo</u>

London July 1954	Philharmonia	Columbia 33CX 1265 Toshiba EAC 37020-38*
London January 1959	Philharmonia	Columbia SAX 2294 EMI SLS 5019*

Grieg

<u>Piano Concerto</u>

London June 1951	Philharmonia Gieseking	Columbia LX 1503/4/5/6 (Auto LX 8888/89/90/91) Columbia 33C 1003 EMI 1C 047 01363M EMI 3C 153 52425-31M* Toshiba EAC 37001-19*
Berlin September 1981	BPO Zimerman	DG 2532 043 <u>DG 410 021-2</u>

<u>Peer Gynt, Suite No 1</u>

Vienna September 1961	VPO	Decca LXT 5673/SXL 2308 Decca JB 16 Decca 417 698-1 <u>Decca 417 722-2</u>
Berlin September 1971	BPO	DG 2530 243 DG 410 981-1 DG 419 474-1
Berlin January and February 1982	BPO	DG 2532 068 <u>DG 410 026-2</u>

<u>Peer Gynt, Suite No 2</u>

Berlin September 1971	BPO	DG 2530 243 DG 410 981-1 DG 419 474-1
Berlin January and February 1982	BPO	DG 2532 068 <u>DG 410 026-2</u>

<u>Ingrid's Lament and Solveig's Song (Peer Gynt, Suite No 2)</u>

Vienna September 1961	VPO	Decca LXT 5673/SXL 2308 Decca JB 16 Decca 417 698-1 <u>Decca 417 722-2</u>

Holberg Suite

Berlin February 1981	BPO	DG 2532 031 DG 400 034-2 DG 419 474-1

Sigurd Jorsalfar, Suite

Berlin September 1971	BPO	DG 2530 243

Gruber

Silent Night (arr. Mohr)

Vienna June 1961	VPO Vienna Singverein Price	Decca LXT 5657/SXL 2294 Decca JB 38

Handel

The Water Music, Suite (arr. Harty)

London November and December 1951	Philharmonia	Columbia unpublished
London April and July 1952	Philharmonia	Columbia LX 8945/6 Columbia 33CX 1033 Toshiba EAC 37001-19*
Berlin December 1959	BPO	Columbia 33CX 1741 Columbia SAX 2389 EMI SLS 839* EMI SXLP 30161 Longanesi Periodici CGL 02

Concerto Grosso Op 6 No 1

St Moritz August 1968	BPO	DG 139 042 DG 2726 068*

Concerto Grosso Op 6 No 2

St Moritz August 1967	BPO	DG 139 035 DG 2726 058*

Concerto Grosso Op 6 No 3

St Moritz August 1967	BPO	DG 139 036 DG 2726 069* DG 2535 269

Concerto Grosso Op 6 No 4

St Moritz August 1967	BPO	DG 139 035 DG 2726 068* DG 2535 269

Concerto Grosso Op 6 No 5

St Moritz August 1966	BPO	DG LPM 19 012/SLPM 139 012 DG 2726 069*

Concerto Grosso Op 6 No 6

St Moritz August 1967	BPO	DG 139 035 DG 2726 068*

Concerto Grosso Op 6 No 7

St Moritz August 1967	BPO	DG 139 036 DG 2726 069*

Concerto Grosso Op 6 No 8

St Moritz August 1968	BPO	DG 139 042 DG 2726 068* DG 2535 269

Concerto Grosso Op 6 No 9

St Moritz August 1967	BPO	DG 139 036 DG 2726 069*

Concerto Grosso Op 6 No 10

St Moritz August 1966	BPO	DG LPM 19 012/SLPM 139 012 DG 2726 069*

Concerto Grosso Op 6 No 11

St Moritz August 1968	BPO	DG 139 042 DG 2726 068*

Concerto Grosso Op 6 No 12

St Moritz August 1966	BPO	DG LPM 19 012/SLPM 139 012 DG 2726 069*

V'adoro pupille (Giulio Cesare)

Berlin September 1960 (Live)	BPO Price	Legendary LR 139

Haydn

Symphony No 82 "The Bear"

Berlin June and September 1980	BPO	DG 2741 005* DG 2532 037 DG 419 741-2*

Symphony No 83 "The Hen"

St Moritz August 1971	BPO	EMI ASD 2817
Berlin June and September 1980	BPO	DG 2741 005* DG 2532 039 DG 419 741-2*

Symphony No 84

Berlin June and September 1980	BPO	DG 2741 005* DG 2532 038 DG 419 741-2*

Symphony No 85 "La Reine"

Berlin June and September 1980	BPO	DG 2741 005* DG 2532 038 DG 419 741-2*

Symphony No 86

Berlin June and September 1980	BPO	DG 2741 006* DG 2532 039 DG 419 741-2*

Symphony No 87

Berlin June and September 1980	BPO	DG 2741 005* DG 2532 037 DG 419 741-2*

Symphony No 93

Berlin January 1982	BPO	DG 2741 015* DG 410 649-1

Symphony No 94 "The Surprise"

Berlin January 1982	BPO	DG 2741 015* DG 410 649-1 DG 410 869-2

Symphony No 95

Berlin January 1982	BPO	DG 2741 015* DG 410 867-1

Deutsche Grammophon Gesellschaft

HERBERT VON KARAJAN
conducting the
Berlin Philharmonic Orchestra

FRANZ LISZT

Hungarian Fantasy for Piano and Orchestra
(with Shura Cherkassky, Piano)
Hungarian Rhapsodies for Orchestra, Nos. 4 & 5
'Mazeppa'—Tone Poem
33 = LPM 18692 (Mono)
33 = SLPM 138 692 (Stereo)

☆

RICHARD STRAUSS

'Ein Heldenleben', Op. 40
33 = LPM 18550 (Mono)
33 = SLPM 138 025 (Stereo)

☆

JOHANNES BRAHMS

Hungarian Dances Nos. 1, 3, 5, 6, 17, 18, 19 & 20

ANTONIN DVORAK

Slavonic Dances Nos. 1, 3, 7, 10 & 16
33 = LPM 18610 (Mono)
33 = SLPM 138 080 (Stereo)

DEUTSCHE GRAMMOPHON (GREAT BRITAIN) LTD.
12/13 RATHBONE PLACE, OXFORD STREET, LONDON, W.1.
Tel.: LANgham 8156/7/8/9

The first LPs for Deutsche Grammophon

Symphony No 96 "The Miracle"

Berlin January 1982	BPO	DG 2741 015*
		DG 410 867-1
		DG 410 975-2

Symphony No 97

Berlin January 1982	BPO	DG 2741 015*
		DG 410 957-1

Symphony No 98

Berlin January 1982	BPO	DG 2741 015*
		DG 410 957-1

Symphony No 99

Berlin January 1982	BPO	DG 2741 015*
		DG 410 958-1

Symphony No 100 "The Military"

Berlin January 1982	BPO	DG 2741 015*
		DG 410 958-1
		DG 410 975-2

Symphony No 101 "The Clock"

Berlin January 1982	BPO	DG 2741 015*
		DG 410 868-1
		DG 410 869-2
St Moritz August 1971	BPO	EMI ASD 2817

Symphony No 102

Berlin January 1982	BPO	DG 2741 015*
		DG 410 868-1

Symphony No 103 "The Drum Roll"

Vienna April 1963	VPO	Decca LXT 6067/SXL 6067
		Decca SDD 312
		Decca SDD 362
		Decca VIV 55
Berlin January 1982	BPO	DG 2741 015*
		DG 410 517-1
		DG 410 517-2

Symphony No 104 "The London"

Vienna March 1959	VPO	RCA RB 16219/SB 2092 Decca SDD 233 Decca SDD 362 Decca VIV 55
Berlin January 1975	BPO	EMI ASD 3203
Berlin January 1982	BPO	DG 2741 015* DG 410 517-1 DG 410 517-2

The Creation

Berlin February 1966 and November 1968	BPO Vienna Singverein Janowitz, C.Ludwig, Wunderlich, Krenn, Fischer-Dieskau, Berry	DG 643 515/6 DG 2707 044 DG 410 951-1
Salzburg August 1982	VPO Vienna Singverein Mathis, Murray, Araiza, Van Dam	DG 2741 017 DG 410 718-2

The Seasons

Berlin November 1972	BPO Choir of Deutsche Oper Janowitz, Hollweg, Berry	EMI SLS 969 Excerpts: EMI EG 29 0567-1 EMI CDM 769 0102

Henrion

The Crusaders, Fanfare (arr. Männeke)

Berlin March 1973	BPO Wind & Brass Ensemble	DG 2721 077* DG 2535 686

Fehrbellin Cavalry March (arr. Männeke)

Berlin March 1973	BPO Wind & Brass Ensemble	DG 2721 077* DG 2535 686 DG 2535 647

Hindemith

Mathis der Maler, Symphony

Berlin October and November 1957	BPO	Columbia 33CX 1783 Columbia SAX 2432 EMI SXLP 30536 EMI 1C 137 54360/1/2/3*

Holst

The Planets

Vienna September 1961	VPO Vienna State Opera Chorus	Decca LXT 5669/SXL 2305 Decca SDD 400 Decca JB 30 Decca 417 709-2
Berlin January and March 1981	BPO RIAS Chamber Choir	DG 2532 019 DG 400 028-2 Excerpt: 415 340-2

Honegger

Symphony No 2

St Moritz August 1969	BPO	DG 2530 068 DG 2543 805

Symphony No 3 "Liturgique"

Berlin September 1969	BPO	DG 2530 068 DG 2543 805

Hopkins

We Three Kings of Orient are

Vienna June 1961	VPO Vienna Singverein Price	Decca LXT 5657/SXL 2294 Decca JB 38

Hummel

Trumpet Concerto in E flat (arr. Oubrados)

Berlin May 1974	BPO André	EMI ASD 3044

Humperdinck

Hansel and Gretel

London June and July 1953	Philharmonia Loughton High School Choir Bancroft's School Choir Schwarzkopf, Grümmer, Ilosvay, Schürhoff, Felbermayer, Metternich	Columbia 33CX 1096/7 World Records OC 187/8 EMI SLS 5145 Excerpts: Columbia 33CX 1819 World Records OH 189

Hansel and Gretel, Overture

Berlin January 1981	BPO	EMI ASD 4072 Toshiba CC28-99008 EMI CDM 769 0202

Kodály

Hary Janos, Intermezzo

London July 1954	Philharmonia	Columbia 33CX 1265 Toshiba EAC 37020-38*
London January 1959	Philharmonia	Columbia unpublished

Komzak

Vindobona March (arr. Mader)

Berlin March 1973   BPO Wind & Brass Ensemble   DG 2721 077*

Archduke Albrecht March (arr. Villinger)

Berlin March 1973   BPO Wind & Brass Ensemble   DG 2721 077*
                                                  DG 2535 467

Lehár

The Merry Widow

Berlin February and   BPO   DG 2707 070
November 1972   Chorus of Deutsche Oper   DG 2725 102
                       Harwood, Stratas, Grobe,   DG 410 921-1
                       Hollweg, Kollo, Kelemen,   DG 415 524-2 (abridged
                       Krenn, Krukowski, Vantin,   without dialogue)
                       Gessendorf, Röhrl, Renar,   Excerpts: DG 2530 729
                       Borris, Pritchett,
                       Grosshans, C.Ott, Reinoso,
                       Trümper

Leimer

Piano Concerto in C minor

London November 1954   Philharmonia   German Columbia WCX 1508
                        Leimer   Electrola SME 91793

Piano Concerto for the Left Hand

London November 1954   Philharmonia   German Columbia WCX 1508
                        Leimer   Electrola SME 91793

Leoncavallo

I Pagliacci

Milan September and   La Scala Orchestra   DG LPM 39 205-7/SLPM 139 205-7*
October 1965   and Chorus   DG 2709 020*
                       Carlyle, Bergonzi, Taddei,   DG 413 275-1*
                       Benelli, Panerai, Morresi,   DG 419 257-2*
                       Ricciardi   Excerpts: DG 136 281
                                                       DG 2535 199

I Pagliacci, Intermezzo

London July 1954	Philharmonia	Columbia 33CX 1265 Toshiba EAC 37020-38*
London January 1959	Philharmonia	Columbia SAX 2294 EMI SLS 5019* EMI SXDW 3048*
Berlin September 1967	BPO	DG 139 031

Lindemann

Under the Flag of Caprice, March (arr. Schmidt)

Berlin March 1973	BPO Wind Ensemble	DG 2721 077*

Liszt

Tasso, Lament and Triumph (Symphonic Poem No 2)

Berlin September 1975	BPO	DG 2530 698 DG 415 628-1* DG 415 967-2*

Les Préludes (Symphonic Poem No 3)

London January 1958	Philharmonia	Columbia 33CX 1548 EMI SLS 5019* EMI SXLP 30450
Berlin April 1967	BPO	DG 139 037 DG 415 628-1* DG 415 967-2*
Berlin December 1983	BPO	DG 413 587-1 DG 413 587-2

Mazeppa (Symphonic Poem No 6)

Berlin December 1960	BPO	DG LPM 18 692/SLPM 138 692 DG 415 628-1* DG 415 967-2*

Hungarian Fantasia for Piano and Orchestra

Berlin December 1960	BPO Cherkassky	DG LPM 18 692/SLPM 138 692 DG 135 031 DG 415 967-2*

Mephisto Waltz

Berlin September 1971	BPO	DG 2530 244 DG 415 628-1* DG 415 967-2*

Hungarian Rhapsody No 2 in C sharp minor

London January 1958	Philharmonia	Columbia 33CX 1571 Columbia SAX 2302 EMI SLS 5019* EMI SXDW 3048*
Berlin April 1967	BPO	DG 139 037 DG 415 628-1* DG 415 967-2*

Hungarian Rhapsody No 4 in E flat

Berlin December 1960	BPO	DG LPM 18 692/SLPM 138 692 DG 135 031 DG 415 628-1*
Berlin October 1975	BPO	DG 2530 698 DG 415 967-2*

Hungarian Rhapsody No 5 in E minor

Berlin December 1960	BPO	DG LPM 18 692/SLPM 138 692 DG 135 031
Berlin October 1975	BPO	DG 2530 698 DG 415 628-1* DG 415 967-2*
Berlin December 1983	BPO	DG 413 587-1 DG 413 587-2

(Note:- Certain changes seem to have occurred in the numbering of these orchestral versions of the Hungarian Rhapsodies in the course of Deutsche Grammophon issuing its various recordings. In the most recent Liszt-Karajan compendiums 415 628-1 (LP) and 415 967-2 (CD) the numbers of Rhapsodies 2 and 4 have become interchanged; whilst in the 1976 issue 2530 698, 4 and 5 have become interchanged. In the above tabulation I have attempted to retain the original numbers, and if, in doing so, I have ignored up-to-date scholarship, I make my apologies to the Liszt experts.)

Locatelli

Concerto Grosso Op 1 No 8 "Christmas Concerto"

St Moritz August 1970	BPO	DG 2530 070 DG 2542 123 DG 415 027-1* DG 419 413-1

Mahler

Symphony No 4

Berlin January and February 1979	BPO Mathis	DG 2531 205 DG 415 323-2

Symphony No 5

Berlin February 1973	BPO	DG 2707 081 DG 415 096-2

Symphony No 6

Berlin September 1977	BPO	DG 2707 106 DG 415 099-2

Symphony No 9

Berlin November 1979, February and September 1980	BPO	DG 2707 125
Berlin September 1982	BPO	DG 410 726-2

Das Lied von der Erde

Berlin December 1973	BPO C.Ludwig, Kollo	DG 2707 082 DG 2531 379 DG 419 058-1

Kindertotenlieder

Berlin May 1974	BPO C.Ludwig	DG 2707 081* DG 2531 147 DG 415 096-2* DG 419 476-1

Rückert-Lieder

Berlin May 1974	BPO C.Ludwig	DG 2707 082* DG 2531 147 DG 415 099-2* DG 419 476-1

Manfredini

Concerto Grosso Op 3 No 12 "Christmas Concerto"

St Moritz August 1970	BPO	DG 2530 070 DG 2542 123 DG 415 027-1* DG 419 046-1 DG 419 413-1 DG 419 046-2

Martin

Etudes for String Orchestra

Berlin May 1958	BPO	Columbia unpublished

Mascagni

Cavalleria Rusticana

Milan September and October 1965	La Scala Orchestra and Chorus Cossotto, Martino, Allegri, Bergonzi, Guelfi	DG LPM 39 205-7/SLPM 139 205-7* DG 2709 020* DG 413 275-1* <u>DG 419 257-2*</u> Excerpts: DG 136 281 DG 2535 199

Cavalleria Rusticana, Intermezzo

Vienna January 1949	VPO	Columbia LX 1208 Columbia SCD 2084
London July 1954	Philharmonia	Columbia 33CX 1265 Toshiba EAC 37020-38*
London January 1959	Philharmonia	Columbia unpublished
Berlin September 1967	BPO	DG 139 031 DG 415 856-1 <u>DG 415 856-2</u>

L'Amico Fritz, Intermezzo

London July 1954	Philharmonia	Columbia 33CX 1265 Toshiba EAC 37020-38*
London January 1959	Philharmonia	Columbia SAX 2294 EMI SLS 5019*
Berlin September 1967	BPO	DG 139 031 DG 415 856-1 <u>DG 419 257-2*</u>, <u>DG 415 856-2</u>
Berlin January 1981	BPO	EMI ASD 4072 <u>Toshiba CC28-99008</u> <u>EMI CDM 769 0202</u>

Massenet

Thaïs, Méditation

London July 1954	Philharmonia Parikian	Columbia 33CX 1265 Toshiba EAC 37020-38*
Berlin September 1967	BPO Schwalbé	DG 139 031 DG 415 856-1 <u>DG 419 257-2*</u>, <u>DG 415 856-2</u>
Berlin January 1981	BPO Mutter	EMI ASD 4072 <u>Toshiba CC28-99008</u> EMI EG 29 10581 <u>EMI CDM 769 0202</u>

Mendelssohn

Symphony No 1

Berlin September 1972	BPO	DG 2720 086*
		DG 2707 084*
		DG 2720 098*

Symphony No 2 "Hymn of Praise"

Berlin September 1972	BPO	DG 2720 086*
	Choir of Deutsche Oper	DG 2707 084
	Mathis, Rebmann, Hollweg	DG 2720 098*

Symphony No 3 "Scotch"

Berlin January 1971	BPO	DG 2720 086*
		DG 2530 126
		DG 2720 098*
		DG 419 477-1

Symphony No 4 "Italian"

Berlin January and February 1971	BPO	DG 2720 086*
		DG 2530 416
		DG 2720 098*
		DG 2543 511
		DG 415 848-1
		DG 415 848-2

Symphony No 5 "Reformation"

Berlin February 1972	BPO	DG 2720 086*
		DG 2530 416
		DG 2720 098*
		DG 2543 511

Violin Concerto

Berlin September 1980	BPO	DG 2532 016
	Mutter	DG 400 031-2

The Hebrides, Overture

Berlin September 1960	BPO	Columbia 33CX 1791
		Columbia SAX 2439
		World Records ST 639
		EMI SXLP 30210
		EMI SXDW 3048*
		EMI EMX 41 2052-1
Berlin January 1971	BPO	DG 2530 126
		DG 2535 310
		DG 419 477-1

54

Hark, the herald angels sing

Vienna June 1961   VPO   Decca LXT 5657/SXL 2294
                            Vienna Singverein   Decca JB 38
                            Price

Moltke

The Great Elector's Cavalry March

Berlin March 1973   BPO Wind & Brass Ensemble   DG 2721 077*
                                                                           DG 2535 586

Leopold Mozart

Toy Symphony (Cassation in G)

London April 1957   Philharmonia   Columbia 33CX 1559
                                           Columbia SAX 2375
                                           EMI SLS 839*
                                           EMI SXLP 30161

Mozart

Symphony No 29

Berlin February and   BPO   Columbia 33CX 1703
March 1960   Columbia SAX 2356
                                           World Records ST 1032
                                           EMI RLS 768*

St Moritz August 1965   BPO   DG LPM 39 002/SLPM 139 002
                                           DG 2535 155

Symphony No 32

Berlin October 1977   BPO   DG 2740 189*
                                         DG 2531 136

Symphony No 33

Vienna October 1946   VPO   Columbia LX 1006/7/8
                                         (Auto LX 8568/9/70)
                                         American Columbia ML 54370
                                         Toshiba EAC 30107

St Moritz August 1965   BPO   DG LPM 39 002/SLPM 139 002
                                           DG 2535 155

Symphony No 35 "Haffner"

Turin 1942	EIAR Turin Orchestra	Polydor 67986/7/8 (Auto 69104/5/6) Cetra RR 8035/6/7 American Decca DL 9513
London November 1954 and May 1955 (previous sessions November and December 1952)	Philharmonia	Columbia 33CX 1511 Toshiba EAC 37001-19*
Washington February 1955 (Live)	BPO	Fonit Cetra LO 506* Maestri del Secolo APE 1201 Movimento Musica 01.003 WG Records WG 30004
Berlin September 1970	BPO	EMI SLS 809* EMI ASD 3016 EMI EG 29 12901 <u>EMI CDM 769 0122</u>
Berlin September 1977	BPO	DG 2740 189* DG 2531 136

Symphony No 36 "Linz"

Berlin September 1970	BPO	EMI SLS 809* EMI ASD 2918
Berlin October 1977	BPO	DG 2740 189* DG 2531 136 DG 410 840-1

Symphony No 38 "Prague"

Vienna September 1958	Philharmonia	Columbia 33CX 1703 Columbia SAX 2356 World Records ST 1032
Berlin September 1970	BPO	EMI SLS 809* EMI ASD 2918
Berlin September 1977	BPO	DG 2740 189* DG 2531 137 DG 410 840-1 DG 419 478-1

Symphony No 39

Vienna October and November 1949	VPO	Columbia LX 1375/6/7 (Auto LX 8785/6/7) American Columbia RL 3068 Toshiba EAC 30107
London July and October 1955	Philharmonia	Columbia 33CX 1361 Toshiba EAC 37001-19*
Berlin September 1970	BPO	EMI SLS 809* EMI ASD 3016 Rehearsal extract: EMI SLS 809*
Berlin September 1977	BPO	DG 2740 189* DG 2531 137 DG 419 478-1

Symphony No 40

Turin 1942	EIAR Turin Orchestra	Polydor 67983/4/5 (Auto 69171/2/3)
Vienna March 1959	VPO	RCA RB 16219/SB 2092 Decca SDD 233 Decca SDD 361 Decca VIV 6 Decca 417 695-1
Berlin September 1970	BPO	EMI SLS 809* EMI ASD 2732 Toshiba CC28-99001 EMI EG 29 12901 EMI CDi1 769 0122 Rehearsal extract: EMI SLS 809*
Berlin September 1977	BPO	DG 2740 198* DG 2531 138

Symphony No 41 "Jupiter"

Turin 1942	EIAR Turin Orchestra	Polydor 67993/4/5/6 (Auto 69363/4/5/6)
London August 1953	Philharmonia	Columbia unpublished (Recording probably incomplete)
Berlin January 1956 (Live)	BPO	Fonit Cetra LO 531 Maestri del Secolo APE 1201 Movimento Musica 01.003 WG Records WG 30004
Vienna May 1962	VPO	Decca LXT 6067/SXL 6067 Decca SDD 312 Decca SDD 361 Decca VIV 6 Decca 417 695-1
Berlin September 1970	BPO	EMI SLS 809* EMI ASD 3732 <u>Toshiba CC28-99001</u> EMI EG 29 12901 <u>EMI CDM 769 0122</u> Rehearsal extract: EMI SLS 809*
Berlin September 1977	BPO	DG 2740 189* DG 2531 138

Piano Concerto No 20

Berlin January 1956 (Live)	BPO Kempff	Fonit Cetra LO 531 Foyer FO 1034*

Piano Concerto No 21

Lucerne August 1950	Lucerne Festival Orchestra Lipatti	Columbia 33C 1064 EMI RLS 749* EMI 2C 051 03713

Piano Concerto No 23

London June 1951	Philharmonia Gieseking	Columbia LX 1510/1/2/3 (Auto LX 8894/5/6/7) Columbia 33C 1012 EMI 3C 153 52425-31M* Toshiba EAC 37001-19*

Piano Concerto No 24

London August 1953	Philharmonia Gieseking	Columbia 33CX 1526 EMI 3C 153 52425-31M* Toshiba EAC 37001-19*

Horn Concertos Nos 1, 2, 3 and 4

London November 1953	Philharmonia Brain	Columbia 33CX 1140 EMI ASD 1140 Toshiba EAC 37001-19* EMI 2C 051 00414
St Moritz August 1968	BPO Seifert	DG 139 038 DG 419 057-1

Bassoon Concerto

St Moritz August 1971	BPO Piesk	EMI SLS 817* EMI ASD 2916 EMI EG 29 12841 EMI CDM 769 0142

Clarinet Concerto

Vienna November 1949	VPO Wlach	German Columbia LWX 445/6/7/8 Toshiba EAC 30108
London July 1955	Philharmonia Walton	Columbia 33CX 1361 Toshiba EAC 37001-19* EMI XLP 60004
St Moritz August 1971	BPO Leister	EMI SLS 817* EMI ASD 2916 EMI EG 29 12841 EMI CDM 769 0142

Flute Concerto No 1

St Moritz August 1971	BPO Blau	EMI SLS 817* EMI ASD 2993 EMI EG 29 0304-1

Flute and Harp Concerto

St Moritz August 1971	BPO Galway Helmis	EMI SLS 817* EMI ASD 2993 EMI EG 29 0304-1

Oboe Concerto

St Moritz August 1971	BPO Koch	EMI SLS 817* EMI ASD 3191 EMI EG 29 12841 EMI CDM 769 0142

Violin Concerto No 3

Berlin December 1977	BPO Mutter	DG 2531 049 DG 410 982-1 DG 415 327-2

Violin Concerto No 5

Berlin September 1972 (Live)	European Youth Orchestra Oistrakh	Melodiya C10 17501-4*
Berlin December 1977	BPO Mutter	DG 2531 049 DG 410 982-1 DG 415 327-2

Sinfonia Concertante for Winds in E flat

London November 1953	Philharmonia Sutcliffe, James, Walton, Brain	Columbia 33CX 1178 Toshiba EAC 37001-19* EMI XLP 60004 EMI RLS 7715*
St Moritz August 1971	BPO Steins, Braun, Stähr, Hauptmann	EMI SLS 817* EMI ASD 3191

String Divertimento No 1 K136/125a

St Moritz August 1967	BPO	DG 139 033 DG 2726 031* DG 2535 259 DG 410 841-1 DG 419 356-1*

String Divertimento No 2 K137/125b

St Moritz August 1967	BPO	DG 139 033 DG 2726 031* DG 2535 259 DG 410 841-1 DG 419 356-1*

String Divertimento No 3 K138/125c

St Moritz August 1967	BPO	DG 139 033 DG 2726 031* DG 2535 259 DG 410 841-1 DG 419 356-1*

Divertimento No 10 K247

St Moritz August 1966	BPO	DG LPM 39 013/SLPM 139 013 DG 2726 031* DG 419 356-1*

Divertimento No 11 K251

St Moritz August 1966	BPO	DG LPM 39 013/SLPM 139 013 DG 2726 031* DG 419 356-1*

Divertimento No 15 K287

London May 1955 (previous sessions in April and May 1952)	Philharmonia	Columbia 33CX 1511 Toshiba EAC 37001-19*
St Moritz August 1965	BPO	DG LPM 39 004/SLPM 139 004 DG 2726 032*

Divertimento No 17 K334

St Moritz August 1965	BPO	DG LPM 39 008/SLPM 139 008 DG 2726 032*

Adagio (Divertimento No 17)

Vienna October 1946 and December 1947	VPO	Columbia unpublished

Minuet (Divertimento No 17)

London July 1955	Philharmonia	Columbia unpublished

Serenade No 6 "Serenata Notturna"

St Moritz August 1967	BPO	DG 139 033 DG 2726 031* DG 2535 259 DG 410 841-1 DG 419 356-1*
Berlin September 1983	BPO	DG 413 309-1 DG 413 309-2

Serenade No 13 "Eine kleine Nachtmusik"

Vienna October 1946	VPO	Columbia LX 1293/4 American Columbia ML 54370 Toshiba EAC 30108
London November 1953	Philharmonia	Columbia 33CX 1178 Toshiba EAC 37001-19*
Berlin December 1959	BPO	Columbia 33CX 1741 Columbia SAX 2389 EMI SLS 839* EMI SXLP 30161 Longanesi Periodici CGL 02
St Moritz August 1965	BPO	DG LPM 39 004/SLPM 139 004 DG 2726 032* DG 2535 259 DG 410 841-1
Berlin February 1981	BPO	DG 2532 031 DG 400 034-2

Masonic Funeral Music

Vienna December 1947   VPO   Columbia LX 1155
                                                      Toshiba EAC 30108

Adagio and Fugue in C minor

Vienna December 1947   VPO   Columbia LX 1076
                                                      American Columbia ML 54370
                                                      Toshiba EAC 30108
                                                      EMI RLS 7714*

St Moritz August 1969   BPO   DG 2530 066

German Dance No 3 "Hurdy-Gurdy" (Four German Dances K602)

Berlin November 1960   BPO   Columbia 33CX 1741
                                                      Columbia SAX 2389
                                                      Longanesi Periodici CGL 02

German Dance No 3 "Sleighride" (Three German Dances K605)

Vienna October 1946   VPO   Columbia unpublished

Berlin November 1960   BPO   Columbia 33CX 1741
                                                      Columbia SAX 2389
                                                      EMI SLS 839*
                                                      EMI SXLP 30161
                                                      Longanesi Periodici CGL 02

German Dance No 5 "Canary" (Six German Dances K600)

Vienna October 1946   VPO   Columbia unpublished

Berlin November 1960   BPO   Columbia 33CX 1741
                                                      Columbia SAX 2389
                                                      Longanesi Periodici CGL 02

Ave verum corpus

Vienna July 1955   Philharmonia   Columbia 33CX 1741
                         Vienna Singverein   Columbia SAX 2389
                                                      EMI SLS 839*
                                                      EMI SXLP 30161
                                                      Longanesi Periodici CGL 02

Mass No 16 "Coronation"

Berlin September 1975	BPO Vienna Singverein Tomowa-Sintow, Baltsa, Krenn, Van Dam	DG 2530 704 DG 2531 342
Rome June 1985 (performed in the framework of Solemn High Mass in St Peter's)	VPO Vienna Singverein Battle, T.Schmidt, Winbergh, Furlanetto	DG 419 096-1 DG 419 096-2

Mass No 18 "Great C Minor"

Berlin February 1981	BPO Vienna Singverein Hendricks, Perry, Schreier, Luxon	DG 2532 028 DG 400 067-2

Mass No 19 "Requiem"

Salzburg August 1960 (Live)	VPO Vienna Singverein Price, Rössl-Majdan, Wunderlich, Berry	HRE Records HRE 317 Movimento Musica 01.023
Berlin October 1961	BPO Vienna Singverein Lipp, Rössl-Majdan, Dermota, Berry	DG LPM 18 767/SLPM 138 767 DG 2535 257
Berlin September 1975	BPO Vienna Singverein Tomowa-Sintow, Baltsa, Krenn, Van Dam	DG 2530 705
Vienna May and June 1986	VPO Vienna Singverein Tomowa-Sintow, Müller-Molinari, Cole, Burchuladze	DG 419 610-1 DG 419 610-2

Alleluja (Exsultate, jubilate)

Vienna June 1961	VPO Price	Decca LXT 5657/SXL 2294 Decca JB 38

Così fan tutte

London July and November 1954	Philharmonia Chorus Schwarzkopf, Merriman, Otto, Simoneau, Panerai, Bruscantini	Columbia 33CX 1262/3/4 World Records SOC 195/6/7 EMI 1C 147 01748/9/50M EMI 1C 197 54200-8M* EMI RLS 7709 Excerpts: World Records OH 198

Don Giovanni

Salzburg August 1960 (Live)	VPO Vienna State Opera Chorus Schwarzkopf, Price, Sciutti, Valletti, Wächter, Zaccaria, Berry, Panerai	HRE Records HRE 247 Movimento Musica 03.001 Movimento Musica 013.6012

(Overture from this performance also on Foyer FO 1034*)

Berlin January 1985	BPO Chorus of Deutsche Oper Baltsa, Tomowa-Sintow, Battle, Winbergh, Ramey, Burchuladze, Furlanetto, Malta	DG 419 179-1 DG 419 179-2 Excerpts: DG 419 635-1 DG 419 635-2

Là ci darem la mano (Don Giovanni)

Vienna December 1947	VPO Seefried, Kunz	EMI RLS 764* EMI 29 12363*
London July 1955	Philharmonia Gobbi Soprano unidentified	Columbia unpublished

Batti, batti (Don Giovanni)

Vienna December 1947	VPO Seefried	Columbia LB 76 EMI RLS 764* EMI 29 12363*

Or sai chi l'onore (Don Giovanni)

Vienna December 1947 (original issue incorrectly stated conductor to be Felix Prohaska)	VPO Cebotari	Electrola WDLP 563 Preiser PR 9860
Vienna December 1948	VPO Welitsch	Columbia unpublished

Crudele ! .... Non mi dir (Don Giovanni)

Vienna December 1947 (original issue incorrectly stated conductor to be Felix Prohaska)	VPO Cebotari	HMV DB 6738 Electrola WDLP 563 EMI 1C 147 29118/9M* EMI RLS 764* Preiser PR 9860

Martern aller Arten (Die Entführung aus dem Serail)

Vienna October 1946	VPO Schwarzkopf	Saga XIG 8011/FID 2143 EMI RLS 763* EMI RLS 7714*

Le Nozze di Figaro

Vienna June and October 1950	VPO Vienna State Opera Chorus Schwarzkopf, Seefried, Jurinac, Höngen, Schwaiger, Czeska, Felbermayer, Kunz, London, Majkut, Rus, Felden	German Columbia LWX 410-425 Columbia 33CX 1007/8/9 EMI 1C 147 01751/2/3M EMI 1C 197 54200-8M* Excerpts: Columbia 33CX 1558 EMI RLS 684*
Milan February 1954 (Live)	La Scala Orchestra and Chorus Schwarzkopf, Seefried, Jurinac, Villa, Adani, Panerai, Petri, Maionica, Pirino, Calabrese, Nessi	Fonit Cetra LO 70 Excerpts: Longanesi Periodici GML 30

(Overture from this performance also on Foyer FO 1034*)

Salzburg July 1974 (Live)	VPO Vienna State Opera Chorus Harwood, Freni, Stade, Berbié, Schary, Spiluttini, Van Dam, Krause, Sénéchal, Montarsolo, Kelemen, Caron	Estro Armonico EA 010
Vienna April and May 1978	VPO Vienna State Opera Chorus Tomowa-Sintow, Cotrubas, Stade, Barbaux, Lambriks, Berbié, Van Dam, Krause, Zednik, Equiluz, Bastin, Kelemen	Decca D132 D4 Excerpts: Decca SXL 6987

Le Nozze di Figaro, Overture

Vienna October 1946	VPO	Columbia LX 1008/LX 8568 Toshiba EAC 30107 EMI RLS 7714*

Non più andrai (Le Nozze di Figaro)

Vienna December 1947	VPO Kunz	Columbia LX 1123 EMI 1C 147 03580-1M* EMI RLS 764*
London July 1955	Philharmonia Gobbi	Columbia unpublished

Se vuol ballare (Le Nozze di Figaro)

Vienna December 1948	VPO Kunz	Columbia unpublished

Voi che sapete (Le Nozze di Figaro)

Vienna December 1947	VPO Seefried	Columbia LB 76 EMI RLS 764* EMI 29 12363*

Deh vieni, non tardar (Le Nozze di Figaro)

Vienna December 1947	VPO Seefried	Columbia LX 1145 EMI RLS 764* EMI 29 12363*

Avanti, avanti, signor uffiziale....Voi che sapete (Le Nozze di Figaro)

Milan December 1948 and January 1949 (Live)	VPO Cebotari, Seefried, Jurinac	Melodram MEL 089*

Signore, di fuori son già suonatori (Le Nozze di Figaro)

Milan December 1948 and January 1949 (Live)	VPO Cebotari, Seefried, Taddei, Höfermayer	Melodram MEL 087*

Ah! la cieca gelosia (Le Nozze di Figaro)

Milan December 1948 and January 1949 (Live)	VPO Schwarzkopf, Seefried, Höfermayer	Melodram MEL 088*

Die Zauberflöte

Vienna November 1950	VPO Vienna Singverein Seefried, Lipp, Loose, Rieger, Jurinac, Stückl, Schürhoff, Steinmassl Dörpinhans, Dermota, Weber, Kunz, London, Klein, Majkut, Pröglhöf	German Columbia LWX 426-444 Columbia 33CX 1013/4/5 EMI SLS 5052 EMI 1C 197 54200-8M* Excerpts: Columbia 33CX 1572 EMI RLS 684*
Vienna May 1962 (Live)	VPO Vienna State Opera Chorus Lipp, Hallstein, Sciutti, Scheyrer, Hofmann, Rössl-Majdan, Gedda, Frick, Kunz, Wächter, Kuen, Lorenzi, Paskalis, Guthrie	Movimento Musica 03.015

(Overture from this performance also on Foyer FO 1034*)

Berlin January and April 1980	BPO Chorus of Deutsche Oper Mathis, K.Ott, Perry, Tomowa-Sintow, Baltsa, Schwarz, Araiza, Hornik, Van Dam, Nicolai, Kruse, Hopfner, Valenta, Horn, Halem, Bünten, Schulz, Pfülb, Quadflieg	DG 2741 001 DG 410 967-2 Excerpts: DG 2532 004 DG 415 287-2

Die Zauberflöte, Overture

Berlin 1938	Berlin Staatskapelle	Polydor 67465 Decca Polydor LY 6145 DG 2810 076

Bei Männern, welche Liebe fühlen (Die Zauberflöte)

Vienna December 1947	VPO Schwarzkopf, Kunz	Columbia unpublished

Mühlberger & Depolo

The Emperor's Marksmen, March (arr. Tanzer)

Berlin March 1973	BPO Wind & Brass Ensemble	DG 2721 077*

Mussorgsky

Boris Godunov (orch. Rimsky-Korsakov)

Vienna November 1970	VPO Vienna State Opera Chorus Vienna Boys Choir Sofia Radio Chorus Ghiaurov, Vishnevskaya, Miljakovic, Dobrianova, Cvejic, Lilowa, Talvela, Masslenikov, Spiess, Markov, Radev, Heppe, Prilcec, Diakov, Paunov, Kelemen, Frese, Karolidis	Decca SET 514/5/6/7 Excerpts: Decca SET 557

Varlaam's Song (Boris Godunov, orch. Rimsky-Korsakov)

London November 1949	Philharmonia Christoff	HMV DB 21097 HMV BLP 1003 EMI 1C 147 03336-7M* EMI RLS 735*

Khovantschina, Entr'acte Act 4 (orch. Rimsky-Korsakov)

London July 1954	Philharmonia	Columbia 33CX 1265 Toshiba EAC 37020-38*
London January 1959	Philharmonia	Columbia SAX 2294 EMI SXLP 30445
Berlin September 1967	BPO	DG 139 031 DG 415 486-1 DG 415 856-2

Dance of the Persian Slaves (Khovantschina, orch. Rimsky-Korsakov)

London November 1954	Philharmonia	Columbia 33CX 1327 Toshiba EAC 37020-38*
London September 1960	Philharmonia	Columbia 33CX 1774 Columbia SAX 2421 EMI SLS 839* EMI SXLP 30200 EMI SXLP 30445 EMI EMX 41 2607-1

Pictures at an Exhibition (orch. Ravel)

London October 1955 and June 1956	Philharmonia	Columbia 33CX 1421 Columbia SAX 2261 EMI SLS 5019* EMI SXLP 30445
Berlin September 1965	BPO	DG LPM 39 010/SLPM 139 010
Berlin February 1986	BPO	DG 413 588-1 DG 413 588-2

Nicolai

The Merry Wives of Windsor, Overture

Berlin September 1960	BPO	Columbia 33CX 1791 Columbia SAX 2439 World Records ST 639 EMI SXLP 30210 EMI EMX 41 2052-1

Nielsen

Symphony No 4 "Inextinguishable"

Berlin February 1981	BPO	DG 2532 029 DG 413 313-2

Offenbach

Barbe-Bleue, Overture

Berlin September 1980	BPO	DG 2532 006
		DG 400 044-2

La Belle Hélène, Overture

Berlin September 1980	BPO	DG 2532 006
		DG 400 044-2

Les Contes d'Hoffmann, Barcarolle

London July 1954	Philharmonia	Columbia 33CX 1265
		Toshiba EAC 37020-38*
London January 1959	Philharmonia	Columbia SAX 2294
		EMI SLS 839*
Berlin September 1980	BPO	DG 2532 006
		DG 400 044-2
		DG 419 469-1

La Grande-Duchesse de Gerolstein, Overture

Berlin September 1980	BPO	DG 2532 006
		DG 400 044-2

Orphée aux Enfers, Overture

London July 1955	Philharmonia	Columbia 33CX 1335
		Toshiba EAC 37020-38*
London September 1960	Philharmonia	Columbia 33CX 1758
		Columbia SAX 2404
		World Records ST 838
		EMI SLS 839*
		EMI CFP 40368
Berlin September 1980	BPO	DG 2532 006
		DG 400 044-2
		DG 415 340-2
		DG 419 469-1

Vert-Vert (Kakadu), Overture

Berlin September 1980	BPO	DG 2532 006
		DG 400 044-2

Gaîté Parisienne, Ballet Suite (orch. Rosenthal)

London January 1958	Philharmonia	Columbia 33CX 1588 Columbia SAX 2274 World Records ST 1084 EMI SLS 5019* EMI SXLP 30224
Berlin January and February 1971	BPO	DG 2530 199 DG 413 983-1

Orff

De temporum fine comoedia

Cologne July 1973   Cologne Radio Orchestra   DG 2530 432
Cologne Radio Chorus
RIAS Chamber Choir
C.Ludwig, Schreier,
Greindl, Boysen, Lorand,
Marsh, Griffel, Anderson,
Killebrew, Lövaas, Loulis,
Tomowa-Sintow, Angervo,
Geisen, Wegmann, Helm,
Anheisser, Frese, Patzalt,
Jokel, Diakov, Carmeli

Pachelbel

Canon and Gigue in D (arr. Seiffert)

St Moritz August 1969	BPO	DG 2530 247 DG 415 201-1 DG 415 301-2 DG 419 046-1 DG 419 488-1 DG 419 046-2
Berlin September 1983	BPO	DG 413 309-1 DG 413 309-2

Piefke

Königgrätz March

Berlin March 1973	BPO Wind & Brass Ensemble	DG 2721 077* DG 2535 647 DG 2535 686

The Glory of Prussia, March

Berlin March 1973	BPO Wind & Brass Ensemble	DG 2721 077* DG 2535 647 DG 2535 686

Ponchielli

Dance of the Hours (La Gioconda)

London November 1954	Philharmonia	Columbia 33CX 1327 Toshiba EAC 37020-38*
London September 1960	Philharmonia	Columbia 33CX 1774 Columbia SAX 2421 EMI SLS 5019*
Berlin December 1970	BPO	DG 2530 200 DG 415 856-1 DG 415 856-2

Prokofiev

Symphony No 1 "Classical"

Berlin February 1981	BPO	DG 2532 031 DG 400 034-2

Symphony No 5

Berlin September 1968	BPO	DG 139 040 DG 410 992-1

Peter and the Wolf

London December 1956 and April 1957	Philharmonia Ustinov (1) Schneider (2) Rothenberger (3) Hirsch (4)	Columbia 33CX 1559 (1) Columbia SAX 2375 (1) German Columbia C70081 (2) Electrola SHZE 243 (3) French Columbia FCX 30531(4)

Puccini

La Bohème

Vienna November 1963 (Live)	VPO Vienna State Opera Chorus Freni, Güden, G.Raimondi, Klein, Taddei, Panerai, Vinco, Frese, Equiluz	Melodram MEL 414 Movimento Musica 02.020 Melodram MEL 27007
Moscow September 1964 (Live)	La Scala Orchestra and Chorus Freni, Vincenzi, G.Raimondi, Panerai, Maffeo, Vinco, Badioli, Calabrese, Forti, Ricciardi, Morresi, Mercuriali	Fonit Cetra CDE 1010 Excerpts: HRE Records HRE 340* Melodram MEL 27007*
Berlin October 1972 and March 1973	BPO Chorus of Deutsche Oper Freni, Harwood, Pavarotti, Sénéchal, Panerai, Maffeo, Ghiaurov, Pohl, Appelt, Pietsch	Decca SET 565/6 Decca 421 049-2 Excerpts: Decca SET 579

Mi chiamano Mimì (La Bohème)

Vienna November 1948	VPO Schwarzkopf	EMI ALP 143 5501

Donde lieta uscì (La Bohème)

Vienna November 1948	VPO Schwarzkopf	Columbia unpublished

Quando men vo (La Bohème)

Vienna November 1948	VPO Welitsch	Columbia LB 82 EMI HLM 7006 World Records SH 289

Madama Butterfly

Milan August 1955	La Scala Orchestra and Chorus Callas, Danieli, Villa Gedda, Ercolani, Carlin, Borriello, Clabassi, Campi	Columbia 33CX 1296/7/8 EMI SLS 5015 EMI EX 29 12653 EMI CDS 747 9598 Excerpts: Columbia 33CX 1787
Vienna January 1974	VPO Vienna State Opera Chorus Freni, C.Ludwig, Schary, Pavarotti, Kerns, Sénéchal, Rintzler, Helm, Stendoro, Scheider, Frese, Hurdes, Mühlberger, Heigl	Decca SET 584/5/6 Decca 417 577-2 Excerpts: Decca SET 605

O mio babbino caro (Gianni Schicchi)

Vienna November 1948	VPO Schwarzkopf	Columbia LB 85 Toshiba EAC 30112 EMI RLS 763*

Suor Angelica, Intermezzo

Berlin September 1967	BPO	DG 139 031 DG 419 257-2*
Berlin January 1981	BPO	EMI ASD 4072 Toshiba CC28-99008 EMI CDM 769 0202

Manon Lescaut, Act 3 Intermezzo

Vienna December 1947 and November 1948	VPO	Columbia LX 1208 Toshiba EAC 30112
London July 1954	Philharmonia	Columbia 33CX 1265 Toshiba EAC 37020-38*
London January 1959	Philharmonia	Columbia SAX 2294 EMI SLS 5019*
Berlin September 1967	BPO	DG 139 031 DG 419 257-2*
Berlin January 1981	BPO	EMI ASD 4072 Toshiba CC28-99008 EMI CDM 769 0202

Tosca

Vienna September 1962	VPO Vienna State Opera Chorus Price, Di Stefano, Taddei, Cava, Corena, Palma, Weiss, Monreale, Mariotti	RCA RE 5507-8/SER 5507-8 Decca 5BB 123/4 Excerpts: RCA RB 6655/SB 6655
Berlin September 1979	BPO Chorus of Deutsche Oper Ricciarelli, Carreras, R.Raimondi, Hornik, Halem, Zednik, Corena, Bünten	DG 2707 121 DG 413 815-2 Excerpts: DG 2537 058

Tosca, Excerpts (Act 1: Mario! Mario!...Ma falle gli occhi neri!; Act 3: Franchigia a Floria Tosca...e mille ti dirò nomi d'amore)

Vienna November 1963 (Live)	VPO Price, Corelli	HRE Records HRE 287*

Turandot

Vienna May 1981	VPO Vienna State Opera Chorus Vienna Boys Choir Ricciarelli, Domingo, Hendricks, De Palma, Hornik, R.Raimondi, Zednik, Araiza, Nimsgern	DG 2741 013 DG 410 096-2 Excerpts: DG 410 645-1 DG 410 645-2

Tu che di gel sei cinta (Turandot)

Vienna November 1948	VPO Schwarzkopf	Columbia unpublished

Rachmaninov

Piano Concerto No 2

Berlin September 1972	BPO Weissenberg	EMI ASD 2872

Radecke

Grenadiers of Fridericus Rex, March

Berlin March 1973	BPO Wind & Brass Ensemble	DG 2721 077* DG 2535 647 DG 2535 686

Ravel

Alborada del Gracioso

Paris June 1971	Orchestre de Paris	EMI ASD 2766 EMI SXLP 30446

Bolero

Berlin September 1965	BPO	DG LPM 39 010/SLPM 139 010 DG 2542 116 DG 413 983-1
Berlin January 1977	BPO	EMI ASD 3431 EMI EG 29 08561 Toshiba CC28-99007 EMI CDM 769 0072
Berlin December 1985	BPO	DG 413 588-1 DG 413 588-2

Daphnis et Chloé, Suite No 2

Berlin March 1964	BPO	DG LPM 18 923/SLPM 138 923
Berlin December 1985 and February 1986	BPO	DG 413 589-1 DG 413 589-2

Pavane pour une infante défunte

Berlin December 1985 and February 1986	BPO	DG 413 589-1 DG 413 589-2

Le Tombeau de Couperin

Paris June 1971	Orchestre de Paris	EMI ASD 2766 EMI SXLP 30446

<u>Rapsodie Espagnole</u>

London July 1953	Philharmonia	Columbia 33CX 1099 Toshiba EAC 37020-38*
Paris June 1971	Orchestre de Paris	EMI ASD 2766 EMI SXLP 30446
Berlin February 1987	BPO	DG 413 588-1 <u>DG 413 588-2</u>

<u>La Valse</u>

Paris June 1971	Orchestre de Paris	EMI ASD 2766 EMI SXLP 30446

Reger

<u>Variations on a theme of Mozart</u>

Berlin January 1958	BPO	Columbia unpublished

Respighi

<u>The Pines of Rome</u>

London January 1958	Philharmonia	Columbia 33CX 1548 EMI SLS 5019* EMI SXLP 30450
Berlin December 1977	BPO	DG 2531 055 <u>DG 413 822-2</u>

<u>The Fountains of Rome</u>

Berlin December 1977	BPO	DG 2531 055 <u>DG 413 822-2</u>

<u>Ancient Airs and Dances for the Lute, Suite No 3</u>

St Moritz August 1969	BPO	DG 2530 247 <u>DG 413 822-2</u>

Rezniček

<u>Donna Diana, Overture</u>

Vienna December 1947	VPO	Columbia LX 1402 Toshiba EAC 30111 EMI RLS 7714*
London July 1955	Philharmonia	Columbia unpublished (probably incomplete)

Rimsky-Korsakov

Scheherazade

Berlin January 1967	BPO	DG 139 022
		DG 419 063-1
		DG 419 063-2

Rossini

String Sonatas Nos 1, 2, 3 and 6

St Moritz August 1968	BPO	DG 139 041
		DG 2535 187

Il Barbiere di Siviglia, Overture

London March 1960	Philharmonia	Columbia 33CX 1729
		Columbia SAX 2378
		EMI SLS 5019*
		EMI SXDW 3048*
		EMI SXLP 30203
Berlin January 1971	BPO	DG 2530 144
		DG 415 377-2

La Gazza Ladra, Overture

London March 1960	Philharmonia	Columbia 33CX 1729
		Columbia SAX 2378
		EMI SLS 5019*
		EMI SXLP 30203
Berlin January 1971	BPO	DG 2530 144
		DG 415 377-2

Guillaume Tell, Overture

London March 1960	Philharmonia	Columbia 33CX 1729
		Columbia SAX 2378
		EMI SLS 839*
		EMI SXLP 30203
Berlin January 1971	BPO	DG 2530 144
		DG 2535 310
		DG 415 377-2
Berlin December 1983	BPO	DG 413 587-1
		DG 413 587-2
		DG 415 340-2

Guillaume Tell, Ballet Music (Passo a tre e Coro tirolese)

London January 1958	Philharmonia	Columbia 33CX 1588 Columbia SAX 2274 World Records ST 1084

La Scala di Seta, Overture

London March 1960	Philharmonia	Columbia 33CX 1729 Columbia SAX 2378 EMI SXLP 30203
Berlin January 1971	BPO	DG 2530 144

L'Italiana in Algeri, Overture

London March 1960	Philharmonia	Columbia 33CX 1729 Columbia SAX 2378 EMI SXLP 30203
Berlin January 1971	BPO	DG 2530 144

Semiramide, Overture

Turin 1942	EIAR Turin Orchestra	Polydor 68154/5
London March 1960	Philharmonia	Columbia 33CX 1729 Columbia SAX 2378 EMI SXLP 30203
Berlin January 1971	BPO	DG 2530 144 DG 415 377-2

Roussel

Symphony No 4

London November 1949	Philharmonia	Columbia LX 1348/49/50/51 (Auto LX 8763/4/5/6) French Columbia FCX 163 Toshiba EAC 37020-38* EMI XLP 60003

Saint-Saëns

Symphony No 3 "Organ Symphony"

Berlin September 1981	BPO Cochereau	DG 2532 045 DG 400 063-2

Schmidt

Notre Dame, Intermezzo

London January 1959	Philharmonia	Columbia SAX 2294 EMI SLS 5019*
Berlin September 1967	BPO	DG 139 031 DG 415 856-1 DG 419 257-2* DG 415 856-2
Berlin January 1981	BPO	EMI ASD 4072 Toshiba CC28-99008 EMI CDM 769 0202

Schoenberg

Pelleas und Melisande

Berlin January 1974	BPO	DG 2740 014* DG 2530 485

Variations for Orchestra

Berlin January and February 1974	BPO	DG 2740 014* DG 2530 627 DG 415 326-2

Verklärte Nacht

Berlin December 1973	BPO	DG 2740 014* DG 2530 627 DG 2543 510 DG 415 326-2

Schrammel

Vienna For Ever, March (arr. Schmidt-Petersen)

Berlin March 1973	BPO Wind & Brass Ensemble	DG 2721 077* DG 2535 647

Schubert

Symphony No 1

Berlin September 1977 and January 1978	BPO	EMI SLS 5127*

Symphony No 2

Berlin September 1977 and January 1978	BPO	EMI SLS 5127*

Symphony No 3

Berlin September 1977 and January 1978	BPO	EMI SLS 5127*

Symphony No 4 "Tragic"

Berlin September 1977 and January 1978	BPO	EMI SLS 5127*

Symphony No 5

Berlin May 1958	BPO	EMI 1C 137 54360/1/2/3*
Berlin September 1977 and January 1978	BPO	EMI SLS 5127* EMI EG 29 05721 EMI CDM 769 0162

Symphony No 6

Berlin September 1977 and January 1978	BPO	EMI SLS 5127*

Symphony No 8 "Unfinished"

London May 1955	Philharmonia	Columbia 33CX 1349 Toshiba EAC 37001-19* EMI SXLP 30513
Berlin October 1964	BPO	DG LPM 39 001/SLPM 139 001 DG 413 982-1 DG 415 848-1 DG 415 848-2
Berlin January 1975	BPO	EMI ASD 3118 EMI SLS 5127* EMI EG 29 05721 EMI CDM 769 0162

SALZBURGER FESTSPIELE 1963

DER ROSENKAVALIER

KOMÖDIE FÜR MUSIK IN DREI AUFZÜGEN
VON HUGO VON HOFMANNSTHAL

MUSIK VON
RICHARD STRAUSS

DIRIGENT
HERBERT VON KARAJAN

INSZENIERUNG
RUDOLF HARTMANN

BÜHNENBILD
TEO OTTO

KOSTÜME
ERNI KNIEPERT

ORCHESTER
**DIE WIENER PHILHARMONIKER
CHOR DER WIENER STAATSOPER**

R. KIESEL SALZBURG

МИНИСТЕРСТВО КУЛЬТУРЫ СССР
ГОСУДАРСТВЕННЫЙ АКАДЕМИЧЕСКИЙ БОЛЬШОЙ ТЕАТР СССР
ГОСКОНЦЕРТ СССР

5–28
сентября 1964 г.

**ГАСТРОЛИ
В МОСКВЕ
МИЛАНСКОГО ТЕАТРА
ЛА СКАЛА**

5–28
сентября 1964 г.

Д. ПУЧЧИНИ
БОГЕМА

Опера в 4 действиях
Либретто Л. ИЛЛИКА и Д. ДЖАКОЗА

ДЕЙСТВУЮЩИЕ ЛИЦА И ИСПОЛНИТЕЛИ:

Рудольф — Джанни Раймонди
Марсель — Роландо Панераи
Шонар — Джанни Маффео
Коллен — Иво Винко
Бенуа — Карло Бадиоли
Альциндор — Франко Калабрезе
Мими — Мирелла Френи
Мюзетта — Зада Винчченца
Парпиньоль — Франко Риччарди
Таможенный сержант — Джузеппе Морреси
Таможенник — Карло Форти
Торговец — Анджело Меркуриали

Дирижер — Герберт фон Караян
Режиссер — Франко Дзеффирелли
Главный художник — Николай Бенуа   Хореограф — Роберто Бенальо
Де́коратор — Франко Дзеффирелли
Художник по костюмам — Марсель Эскофье
Ассистент режиссера — Джулио Лупетти

Numerous live performances have found
their way onto unauthorised LPs and CDs,
among them "Der Rosenkavalier" in
Salzburg and "La Bohème" in Moscow

カラヤン〜ウィーン・フィル
24年振りの再録音

カラヤン／ウィーン・フィル
ドヴォルザーク：交響曲第8番

◎ドヴォルザーク
交響曲第8番ト長調 作品88
ウィーン・フィルハーモニー管弦楽団
指揮：ヘルベルト・フォン・カラヤン
CD F35G-20114 ¥3,500
LP 28MG-0960 MC 28CG-0960／各¥2,800
〈デジタル録音〉
〈録音 1985年1月、ウィーン〉
●5月25日発売

LP MC 同時発売

カラヤン／ウィーン・フィル
モーツァルト：レクィエム

好評発売中

◎モーツァルト
レクィエム ニ短調 K.626
アンナ・トモワ＝シントウ（ソプラノ）
ヘルガ・ミュラー＝モリナーリ（アルト）
ヴィンスン・コウル（テノール）
パータ・ブルチュラーゼ（バス）
ウィーン楽友協会合唱団
（合唱指揮 ヘルムート・フロシャウアー）
ウィーン・フィルハーモニー管弦楽団
指揮 ヘルベルト・フォン・カラヤン
CD F35G-20104 ¥3,500
LP 28MG-0956 ¥2,800 〈デジタル録音〉
〈録音 1986年5、6月、ウィーン〉

Recent recordings are presented to the Japanese public, retaining their European flavour to the full

Symphony No 9 "Great"

Vienna September 1946	VPO	Columbia LX 1138/39/40/41/42/43 (Auto LX 8644/5/6/7/8/9) American Columbia ML 54631 Toshiba EAC 30104
Berlin September 1968	BPO	DG 139 043 DG 2535 290 DG 410 980-1
Berlin June 1977	BPO	EMI SLS 5127* EMI EG 29 06121

Rosamunde (The Magic Harp), Overture

Berlin September 1977 and January 1978	BPO	EMI SLS 5127* EMI SXLP 30505

Rosamunde, Ballet Music No 1

Berlin September 1977 and January 1978	BPO	EMI SLS 5127*

Rosamunde, Ballet Music No 2

Berlin September 1977 and January 1978	BPO	EMI SLS 5127*

Ave Maria (arr. Sabatini)

Vienna June 1961	VPO Price	Decca LXT 5657/SXL 2294 Decca JB 38

Schumann

Symphony No 1 "Spring"

Berlin January and February 1971	BPO	DG 2720 046* DG 2530 169 DG 2740 129* DG 419 065-1

Symphony No 2

Berlin February 1971	BPO	DG 2720 046* DG 2530 170 DG 2740 129*

Symphony No 3 "Rhenish"

Berlin February 1971	BPO	DG 2720 046* DG 2530 447 DG 2740 129*

Symphony No 4

Berlin April 1957	BPO	Columbia 33C 1056 EMI 1C 047 01441M EMI RLS 768*
Berlin January and February 1971	BPO	DG 2720 046* DG 2530 169 DG 2740 129* DG 413 982-1 DG 419 065-1

Piano Concerto

London April 1948	Philharmonia Lipatti	Columbia LX 1110/1/2/3 (Auto LX 8624/5/6/7) Columbia 33C 1001 EMI XLP 30072 EMI HLM 7046 Toshiba EAC 37001-19* EMI 2C 051 03713
London August 1953	Philharmonia Gieseking	Columbia 33C 1033 EMI 1C 047 01401M EMI 3C 153 52425-31M* Toshiba EAC 37001-19*
Berlin September 1981	BPO Zimerman	DG 2532 043 DG 410 021-2

Overture, Scherzo and Finale

Berlin February 1971	BPO	DG 2720 046* DG 2530 170 DG 2740 129*

Seifert

Carinthian Songs, March

Berlin March 1973	BPO Wind & Brass Ensemble	DG 2721 077*
		DG 2535 647

Shostakovich

Symphony No 10

Berlin November 1966	BPO	DG 139 020
Moscow May 1969 (Live)	BPO	Melodiya C10 21227 009
Berlin February 1981	BPO	DG 2532 030
		DG 413 361-2

Sibelius

Symphony No 1

Berlin January 1981	BPO	EMI ASD 4097
		Toshiba CC28-99004
		EMI CDM 769 0282

Symphony No 2

London March 1960	Philharmonia	Columbia 33CX 1730
		Columbia SAX 2379
		EMI SXLP 30414
Berlin November 1980	BPO	EMI ASD 4060
		Toshiba CC28-99005

Symphony No 4

London July 1953	Philharmonia	Columbia 33CX 1125
		Toshiba EAC 37020-38*
Berlin September 1965	BPO	DG LPM 18 974/SLPM 138 974
		DG 2720 067*
		DG 2542 128
		DG 2740 255*
		DG 415 108-2
Berlin December 1976	BPO	EMI ASD 3485
		EMI EG 29 06131

Symphony No 5

London December 1951 and July 1952	Philharmonia	Columbia 33CX 1047 Toshiba EAC 37020-38*
London September 1960	Philharmonia	Columbia 33CX 1750 Columbia SAX 2392 EMI SXLP 30430
Berlin February 1965	BPO	DG LPM 18 973/SLPM 138 973 DG 2720 067* DG 2542 109 DG 2740 255* DG 415 107-2
Berlin September and October 1976	BPO	EMI ASD 3409 EMI EG 29 06131

Symphony No 6

London July 1955	Philharmonia	Columbia 33CX 1341 Toshiba EAC 37020-38*
Berlin April 1967	BPO	DG 139 032 DG 2720 067* DG 2542 137 DG 2740 255* DG 415 108-2
Berlin November 1980	BPO	EMI EL 27 04071

Symphony No 7

London July 1955	Philharmonia	Columbia 33CX 1341 Toshiba EAC 37020-38* EMI SXLP 30430
Berlin September 1967	BPO	DG 139 032 DG 2720 067* DG 2542 137 DG 2740 255* DG 415 107-2

Violin Concerto

Berlin October 1964	BPO	DG LPM 18 961/SLPM 138 961 DG 2740 137* DG 2740 255*

En Saga

Berlin September 1976	BPO	EMI ASD 3374 EMI ASD 3409 EMI EL 27 04071 EMI CDM 769 0172

Finlandia

London July 1952	Philharmonia	Columbia LX 1593 Columbia 33CX 1047 Toshiba EAC 37020-38*
London January 1959	Philharmonia	Columbia 33CX 1750 Columbia SAX 2392 EMI SLS 5019*
Berlin October 1964	BPO	DG LPM 18 961/SLPM 138 961 DG LPM 39 016/SLPM 139 016 DG 2542 109 DG 2740 255* DG 410 981-1
Berlin September 1976	BPO	EMI ASD 3374 EMI CDM 769 0172
Berlin February 1984	BPO	DG 413 755-1 DG 413 755-2

Karelia Suite

Berlin January 1981	BPO	EMI ASD 4097 EMI EL 27 04071 Toshiba CC28-99004 EMI CDM 769 0282

Pelléas et Mélisande

Berlin January and February 1982	BPO	DG 2532 068 DG 410 026-2

The Swan of Tuonela

Berlin September 1965	BPO	DG LPM 18 974/SLPM 138 974 DG LPM 39 016/SLPM 139 016 DG 2542 128 DG 2740 255*
Berlin September 1976	BPO	EMI ASD 3374 EMI CDM 769 0172
Berlin February 1984	BPO	DG 413 755-1 DG 413 755-2

Tapiola

London July 1953	Philharmonia	Columbia 33CX 1125 Toshiba EAC 37020-38*
Berlin October 1964	BPO	DG LPM 18 973/SLPM 138 973 DG LPM 39 016/SLPM 139 016 DG 2740 255*
Berlin September 1976	BPO	EMI ASD 3374 EMI ASD 3485 EMI CDM 769 0172
Berlin February 1984	BPO	DG 413 755-1 DG 413 755-2

Valse triste

London January 1958	Philharmonia	Columbia 33CX 1571 Columbia SAX 2302 EMI SLS 5019*
Berlin January 1967	BPO	DG LPM 39 016/SLPM 139 016 DG 2542 109 DG 2740 255* DG 410 981-1
Berlin November 1980	BPO	EMI EL 27 04071
Berlin February 1984	BPO	DG 413 755-1 DG 413 755-2

Smetana

The Moldau (Má Vlast)

Berlin 1940	BPO	Polydor 67583/4 DG LPEM 19 078
Berlin May 1958	BPO	Columbia 33CX 1642 Columbia SAX 2275 EMI SLS 839* EMI ASD 2863 EMI SXDW 3048* EMI SXLP 100 4911
Berlin April 1967	BPO	DG 139 037 DG 2543 509
Berlin January 1977	BPO	EMI ASD 3407 Toshiba CC28-99002 EMI CDM 769 0052
Berlin December 1983	BPO	DG 413 587-1 DG 413 587-2
Vienna May 1985	VPO	DG 415 509-1 DG 415 509-2

Vysherad (Má Vlast)

Berlin April 1967	BPO	DG 139 037

Endlich allein....wie fremd und tot (The Bartered Bride)

Vienna December 1947	VPO Konetzni	Columbia LX 1074 EMI RLS 764*

Polka, Furiant and Dance of the Comedians (The Bartered Bride)

Berlin September 1971	BPO	DG 2530 244 DG 2543 509 Polka only: DG 415 856-1 DG 415 856-2

Sonntag

Nibelungen March (arr. Villinger)

Berlin March 1973	BPO Wind & Brass Ensemble	DG 2721 077*

Sousa

Stars and Stripes Forever, March

London July 1953	Philharmonia	Columbia unpublished

El Capitan, March

London July 1953	Philharmonia	Columbia unpublished

Johann Strauss father

Radetzky March

London July 1955	Philharmonia	Columbia 33CX 1335 Toshiba EAC 37020-38*
Brussels June 1958 (Live)	VPO	Movimento Musica 01.039
London September 1960	Philharmonia	Columbia 33CX 1758 Columbia SAX 2404 World Records ST 838 EMI SXDW 3048* EMI CFP 40368
Berlin December 1966	BPO	DG 139 014 DG 415 852-1
Berlin December 1980	BPO	DG 2741 003* DG 2532 027 DG 410 027-2 DG 415 340-2
Vienna January 1987	VPO	DG 419 616-1 DG 419 616-2

Annen-Polka

Vienna January 1987	VPO	DG 419 616-1
		DG 419 616-2

Johann Strauss

Accelerationen, Waltz

Berlin December 1980	BPO	DG 2741 003*
		DG 2532 025
		DG 400 026-2

Aegyptischer Marsch

Berlin April 1969	BPO	DG 2530 027

An der schönen blauen Donau, Waltz

Vienna October 1946	VPO	Columbia LX 1118
		Toshiba EAC 30110
London July 1955	Philharmonia	Columbia 33CX 1393
		Toshiba EAC 37020-38*
Brussels June 1958 (Live)	VPO Vienna Männergesangverein	Movimento Musica 01.039
Berlin December 1966	BPO	DG 139 014
		DG 2542 143
		DG 415 852-1
Berlin January and December 1975	BPO	EMI ASD 3132
		EMI EG 29 06141
		EMI CDM 769 0182
Berlin December 1980	BPO	DG 2741 003*
		DG 2532 025
		DG 400 026-2
Vienna January 1987	VPO	419 616-1
		419 616-2

Annen Polka

Brussels June 1958 (Live)	VPO		Movimento Musica 01.039
Vienna August 1959	VPO		RCA RB 16216/SB 2091 Decca SDD 259
Berlin December 1966	BPO		DG 139 014 DG 2542 143 DG 415 852-1
Berlin January and December 1975	BPO		EMI ASD 3132 EMI EG 29 06141 EMI CDM 769 0182
Berlin December 1980	BPO		DG 2741 003* DG 2532 006 DG 410 022-2
Vienna January 1987	VPO		419 616-1 419 616-2

Eljen a Magyar, Polka

Berlin December 1980	BPO		DG 2741 003* DG 2532 025 DG 410 026-2

Die Fledermaus

London April 1955		Philharmonia Chorus Schwarzkopf, Streich, Gedda, Krebs, Kunz, Dönch, Christ, Majkut, Böheim, Martinis	Columbia 33CX 1309/10 EMI RLS 728 Excerpts: Columbia 33CX 1516
Vienna July 1960		VPO Vienna State Opera Chorus Güden, Köth, Kmennt, Berry, Wächter, Zampieri, Resnik, Klein, Kunz, Schubert, Godknow, Fasolt, Mattoni	Decca MET 201/2/3 (a) Decca SET 201/2/3 (a) Decca LXT 6015/6 Decca SXL 6015/6 Decca D247 D3 (a) Decca 421 046-2 (a) (a) with gala sequence not conducted by Karajan Excerpts: Decca LXT 6155/SXL 6155 Ballet music only: Decca ADD 150/SDD 150
Vienna December 1960 (Live)		VPO Vienna State Opera Chorus Güden, Streich, Wächter, Kunz, Stolze, Zampieri, Berry, Klein, E.Ott, Meinrad	Foyer FO 1031 Excerpts: Longanesi Periodici GML 25

"Die Fledermaus"-Quadrille

Berlin December 1980	BPO		DG 2741 003* DG 2532 027 DG 410 027-2

Die Fledermaus, Overture

Berlin 1942	BPO	Polydor 68043
Vienna December 1948	VPO	Columbia LX 1546 Toshiba EAC 30110
Brussels June 1958 (Live)	VPO	Movimento Musica 01.039
Vienna August 1959	VPO	RCA RB 16216/SB 2091 Decca SDD 259
Berlin December 1966	BPO	DG 139 014 DG 2535 310 DG 2543 533
Berlin January and December 1975	BPO	EMI ASD 3132 EMI EG 29 06141 EMI CDM 769 0182
Berlin December 1980	BPO	DG 2741 003* DG 2532 025 DG 400 026-2
Vienna January 1987	VPO	419 616-1 419 616-2

Frühlingsstimmen, Waltz

Brussels June 1958 (Live)	VPO Güden	Movimento Musica 01.039
Vienna January 1987	VPO Battle	DG 419 616-1 DG 419 616-2

G'schichten aus dem Wienerwald, Waltz

Vienna November 1948	VPO	Columbia LX 1274 Toshiba EAC 30110 EMI RLS 7714*
Vienna August 1959	VPO	RCA RB 16216/SB 2091 Decca SDD 259
Berlin April 1969	BPO	DG 2530 027 DG 2542 143 DG 415 852-1
Berlin December 1980	BPO	DG 2741 003* DG 2532 027 DG 410 027-2

Morgenblätter, Waltz

Berlin April 1969	BPO	DG 2530 027

Napoleon March

Berlin December 1980	BPO	DG 2741 003* DG 2532 027 DG 410 027-2

Auf der Jagd, Polka

Brussels June 1958 (Live)	VPO	Movimento Musica 01.039
Vienna August 1959	VPO	RCA RB 16216/SB 2091 Decca SDD 259
Berlin April 1969	BPO	DG 2530 027 DG 415 852-1
Berlin December 1980	BPO	DG 2741 003* DG 2532 006 DG 410 022-2

Kaiserwalzer

Berlin 1941	BPO	Polydor 67649
Vienna October 1946	VPO	Columbia LX 1021 Toshiba EAC 30111
London July 1955	Philharmonia	Columbia 33CX 1393 Toshiba EAC 37020-38*
Brussels June 1958 (Live)	VPO	Movimento Musica 01.039
Berlin December 1966	BPO	DG 139 014 DG 415 852-1
Berlin January and December 1975	BPO	EMI ASD 3132 EMI EG 29 06141 EMI CDM 769 0182
December 1980	BPO	DG 2741 003* DG 2532 026 DG 410 022-2

Künstlerleben, Waltz

Berlin 1940	BPO	Polydor 67585
Vienna October 1946	VPO	Columbia LX 1012 Toshiba EAC 30111
London May and July 1955	Philharmonia	Columbia 33CX 1393 Toshiba EAC 37020-38*
Berlin December 1980	BPO	DG 2741 003* DG 2532 025 DG 400 026-2

Leichtes Blut, Polka

Vienna October 1946	VPO	Columbia unpublished
Berlin December 1980	BPO	DG 2741 003* DG 2532 025 DG 400 026-2

Ohne Sorgen, Polka

Vienna January 1987	VPO	DG 419 616-1
		DG 419 616-2

Perpetuum mobile

Vienna January 1949	VPO	Columbia LB 128
		Toshiba EAC 30110
		EMI RLS 7714*
Berlin December 1966	BPO	DG 139 014
Berlin December 1980	BPO	DG 2741 003*
		DG 2532 027
		DG 410 027-2

Persischer Marsch

Berlin April 1969	BPO	DG 2530 027
		DG 415 852-1
Berlin December 1980	BPO	DG 2741 003*
		DG 2532 025
		DG 400 026-2

Rosen aus dem Süden, Waltz

Berlin December 1980	BPO	DG 2741 003*
		DG 2532 026
		DG 410 022-2

Tritsch-Tratsch Polka

Vienna October 1949	VPO	Columbia LB 128
		Toshiba EAC 30110
		EMI RLS 7714*
London July 1955	Philharmonia	Columbia 33CX 1335
		Toshiba EAC 37020-38*
London September 1960	Philharmonia	Columbia 33CX 1758
		Columbia SAX 2404
		World Records ST 838
		EMI CFP 40368
Berlin December 1966	BPO	DG 139 014
		DG 2542 143
Berlin January and December 1975	BPO	EMI ASD 3132
		EMI EG 29 06141
		EMI CDM 769 0182
Berlin December 1980	BPO	DG 2741 003*
		DG 2532 026
		DG 410 022-2

Unter Donner und Blitz, Polka

Vienna October 1949	VPO	Austrian Columbia LV 15
London July 1955	Philharmonia	Columbia 33CX 1335 Toshiba EAC 37020-38*
Brussels June 1958 (Live)	VPO	Movimento Musica 01.039
London September 1960	Philharmonia	Columbia 33CX 1758 Columbia SAX 2404 World Records ST 838 EMI CFP 40368
Berlin April 1969	BPO	DG 2530 027 DG 2542 143 DG 415 852-1
Berlin December 1980	BPO	DG 2741 003* DG 2532 025 DG 400 026-2
Vienna January 1987	VPO	DG 419 616-1 DG 419 616-2

Vergnügungszug-Polka

Vienna January 1987	VPO	DG 419 616-1 DG 419 616-2

Wein, Weib und Gesang, Waltz

Vienna October 1949	VPO	Columbia LX 1402 Toshiba EAC 30111
Berlin December 1980	BPO	DG 2741 003* DG 2532 026 DG 410 022-2

Wiener Blut, Waltz

Vienna October and November 1949	VPO	Columbia LX 1321 Toshiba EAC 30111
Berlin April 1969	BPO	DG 2530 027 DG 2542 143 DG 415 852-1
Berlin December 1980	BPO	DG 2741 003* DG 2532 027 DG 410 027-2

Zigeunerbaron March (arr. Villinger)

Berlin March 1973	BPO Wind & Brass Ensemble	DG 2721 077*

So elend und treu....so habet acht (Der Zigeunerbaron)

Vienna November 1948	VPO Cebotari	HMV DB 6947 EMI 1C 147 29118/9M* EMI RLS 764* Preiser PR 9680

Der Zigeunerbaron, Overture

Berlin 1942	BPO	Polydor 67997 BASF 98 22177* Acanta KB 22177*
Vienna October 1946	VPO	Columbia LX 1009 Toshiba EAC 30110
London July 1955	Philharmonia	Columbia 33CX 1393 Toshiba EAC 37020-38*
Vienna August 1959	VPO	RCA RB 16216/SB 2091 Decca SDD 259
Berlin December 1966	BPO	DG 139 014 DG 2543 533
Berlin January and December 1975	BPO	EMI ASD 3132 EMI SXLP 30506 EMI EG 29 06141 EMI CDM 769 0182
Berlin December 1980	BPO	DG 2741 003* DG 2532 006 DG 410 022-2

Johann & Josef Strauss

Pizzicato Polka

Vienna October 1948	VPO	Columbia unpublished
London May and July 1955	Philharmonia	Columbia 33CX 1393 Toshiba EAC 37020-38*
Brussels June 1958 (Live)	VPO	Movimento Musica 01.039
Berlin April 1969	BPO	DG 2530 027 DG 415 852-1
Vienna January 1987	VPO	DG 419 616-1 DG 419 616-2

Josef Strauss

Sphärenklänge, Waltz

Vienna October 1949	VPO	Columbia LX 1250 German Columbia C50143
London January 1958	Philharmonia	Columbia unpublished
Berlin December 1980	BPO	DG 2741 003* DG 2532 027 DG 410 027-2
Vienna January 1987	VPO	DG 419 616-1 DG 419 616-2

Delirienwalzer

Vienna October 1949	VPO	Columbia LX 1303 Toshiba EAC 30111 EMI RLS 7714*
London July 1955	Philharmonia	Columbia 33CX 1393 Toshiba EAC 37020-38*
Vienna August 1959	VPO	RCA RB 16216/SB 2091 Decca SDD 259
Berlin December 1966	BPO	DG 139 014
Berlin December 1980	BPO	DG 2741 003* DG 2532 027 DG 410 027-2
Vienna January 1987 (Live)	VPO	DG 419 616-1 DG 419 616-2

Transaktionen, Waltz

Vienna October 1949	VPO	Columbia LX 1257 German Columbia C50143

Richard Strauss

Also sprach Zarathustra

Vienna March 1959	VPO	Decca LXT 5524/SXL 2154 Decca ADD 175/SDD 175 Decca JB 27 Decca 417 770-2
Berlin January and March 1973	BPO	DG 2530 402 DG 2740 111* DG 415 853-1
Berlin September 1983	BPO	DG 410 959-1 DG 410 959-2

An Alpine Symphony

Berlin December 1980	BPO	DG 2532 015 DG 410 959-2

Don Quixote

Berlin December 1965	BPO Fournier	DG LPM 39 009/SLPM 139 009 DG 2535 195 DG 2740 111*
Berlin January 1975	BPO Rostropovich	EMI ASD 3118 EMI 1C 137 54360/1/2/3*
Berlin January 1986	BPO Meneses	DG 419 599-1 DG 419 599-2

Don Juan

Amsterdam 1943	Concertgebouw	Polydor 68127/8/9 American Decca DL 9529
London December 1951	Philharmonia	Columbia LX 8920/1 Columbia 33CX 1001 Toshiba EAC 37020-38* EMI RLS 7715*
Vienna June 1960	VPO	Decca LXT 5629/SXL 2269 Decca SPA 119 Decca JB 27 Decca 417 770-2
Berlin December 1972	BPO	DG 2530 349 DG 2740 111* DG 410 839-1
Berlin February and November 1983	BPO	DG 410 959-1 DG 410 959-2

Ein Heldenleben

Berlin March 1959	BPO	DG LPM 18 550/SLPM 138 025 DG 2535 194 DG 2740 111*
Salzburg August 1964 (Live)	BPO	Paragon PCD 84008
Berlin May 1974	BPO	EMI ASD 3046 EMI EG 29 08521 Toshiba CC28-99010
Berlin February 1986	BPO	DG 415 508-1 DG 415 508-2

Metamorphosen

Vienna October and November 1947	VPO	Columbia LX 1082/3/4/5 (Auto LX 8606/7/8/9) Toshiba EAC 30109 EMI RLS 7714*
St Moritz August 1969	BPO	DG 2530 066 DG 2740 111*
Berlin September 1980	BPO	DG 2532 074 DG 410 892-2

Sinfonia Domestica

Paris June 1973	BPO	EMI ASD 2955

Till Eulenspiegels lustige Streiche

London December 1951	Philharmonia	Columbia LX 8908/9 Columbia 33CX 1001 Toshiba EAC 37020-38* EMI RLS 7715*
Washington February 1955 (Live)	BPO	Fonit Cetra LO 506* Foyer FO 1034*
Vienna June 1960	VPO	Decca LXT 5620/SXL 2261 Decca SDD 211 Decca JB 27 <u>Decca 417 722-2</u>
Berlin December 1972	BPO	DG 2530 349 DG 2740 111* DG 410 839-1 DG 415 853-1
Berlin January 1986	BPO	DG 419 599-1 <u>DG 419 599-2</u>

Tod und Verklärung

London July 1953	Philharmonia	EMI 2M 055 43228 EMI RLS 7715*
Vienna September 1960	VPO	Decca LXT 5620/SXL 2261 Decca SDD 211 <u>Decca 717 720-2</u>
Berlin November 1972	BPO	DG 2530 368 DG 2740 111* DG 410 839-1
Berlin January 1982	BPO	DG 2532 074 <u>DG 410 892-2</u>

Horn Concerto No 2

Berlin March 1973	BPO Hauptmann	DG 2530 439

Oboe Concerto

Berlin September 1969	BPO Koch	DG 2530 439

Ariadne auf Naxos

London June and July 1954	Philharmonia Schwarzkopf, Seefried, Streich, Otto, Hoffman, Felbermayer, Schock, Neugebauer, Dönch, Unger, Cuenod, Strauss, Kraus, Prey, Ollendorff, Krebs	Columbia 33CX 1292/3/4 EMI RLS 760

Es gibt ein Reich (Ariadne auf Naxos)

Vienna November 1948   VPO
                               Cebotari
                                                 HMV DB 6914
                                                 EMI 1C 147 29118/9M*
                                                 World Records SH 286
                                                 EMI RLS 764*
                                                 Preiser PR 9860

Orchestral Interlude and Closing Scene (Capriccio)

Berlin November 1985   BPO   DG 419 188-1
                                       Tomowa-Sintow   <u>DG 419 188-2</u>
                                       Wolfrum

Elektra

Salzburg August 1964   VPO   Estro Armonico EA 044
(Live)   Vienna State Opera Chorus   Melodram MEL 718
                                       Mödl, Varnay, Hillebrecht,
                                       Rütgers, Haan, Hellwig,
                                       Watts, Sjöstedt, Ahlin,
                                       Otto, Popp, King, Franc,
                                       Wächter, Vrooman, Frese

Salome

Vienna May 1977   VPO   EMI SLS 5139
                                       Behrens, Baltsa, Angervo,   <u>EMI CDS 749 3588</u>
                                       Van Dam, Böhm, Ochman,
                                       Zednik, Knutson, Vantin,
                                       Unger, Kunz, Bastin,
                                       Ellenbeck, Nienstedt,
                                       Rydl, Bömches, Nitsche

<u>Orchestral Interlude (Jochanaan descends into the cistern) and Closing Scene</u>
<u>(excluding the section "Oeffne Deine Augen....hörte ich geheimnisvolle Musik")</u>
<u>(Salome)</u>

Vienna November 1948   VPO   World Records SH 286
                                       Welitsch, Schuster, Witt

Dance of the Seven Veils (Salome)

Amsterdam 1943   Concertgebouw   Polydor 68126

Vienna September 1960   VPO   Decca LXT 5620/SXL 2661
                                                 Decca SDD 211

Berlin December 1972   BPO   DG 2530 349
                                                 DG 2740 111*

Der Rosenkavalier

London December 1956	Philharmonia Chorus Loughton High School Choir Bancroft's School Choir Schwarzkopf, C.Ludwig, Stich-Randall, Welitsch, Meyer, Felbermayer, Kuen, Majkut, Unger, Gedda, Friedrich, Edelmann, Wächter, Bierbach, Pröglhöf	Columbia 33CX 1492/3/4/5 Columbia SAX 2269/70/1/2 EMI SLS 810 EMI EX 29 00453 EMI CDS 749 3548 Excerpts: Columbia 33CX 1777 Columbia SAX 2423
Salzburg July 1963 (Live)	VPO Vienna State Opera Chorus Schwarzkopf, Jurinac, Rothenberger, Hellwig, Plümacher, Dutoit, Küster, Nessel, La Bruce, Romani, Ercolani, Edelmann, Dönch, Equiluz, Pernerstorfer, Häusler, Frese, Knapp, Sperlbauer, Mayer, Stumper, Vajda, Buchbauer, Sengl, Resch, Bernhard, Balatsch	Movimento Musica 04.004
Vienna November and December 1982, May 1983 and January 1984	VPO Concert Association of Vienna State Opera Chorus Tomowa-Sintow, Baltsa Perry, Lipp, Müller-Molinari, Sima, Poschner, Winsauer, Hintermeier, Cole, Zednik, Equiluz, Moll, Hornik, Halem, Kasemann, Feller, Terkal, Nitsche, Tomaschek, Reinprecht, Scheider, Panzenböck, Koblitz, Zeh, Holzherr, Lichtenberger, Reautschnigg	DG 413 163-1 DG 413 163-2 Excerpts: DG 415 284-1 DG 415 284-2

Marschallin's Monologue & Quinquin, er soll jetzt gehn (Der Rosenkavalier)

Vienna December 1947	VPO Konetzni	Columbia LX 1135

Presentation of the Silver Rose (Der Rosenkavalier)

Vienna December 1947	VPO Schwarzkopf, Seefried	Columbia LX 1225/6 American Columbia ML 2126 World Records SH 286 EMI RLS 763* EMI RLS 7714*

Der Rosenkavalier, Suite No 1

London January 1958	Philharmonia	Columbia unpublished

Vier letzte Lieder

Salzburg August 1964 (Live)	BPO Schwarzkopf	Paragon PCD 84008
Berlin February 1973	BPO Janowitz	DG 2530 368
Berlin November 1985	BPO Tomowa-Sintow	DG 419 188-1 DG 419 188-2

Die heiligen drei Könige

Berlin November 1985	BPO Tomowa-Sintow	DG 419 188-1 DG 419 188-2

Stravinsky

Apollon Musagète

St Moritz August 1969	BPO	DG 2530 065 DG 2542 134 DG 415 979-2

Circus Polka

Berlin April 1970	BPO	DG 2530 267

Concerto in D for strings

St Moritz August 1969	BPO	DG 2530 267

Jeu de cartes

London May 1952	Philharmonia	French Columbia FCX 163 Toshiba EAC 37020-38* EMI XLP 60003

Le sacre du printemps

Berlin November 1963	BPO	DG LPM 18 920/SLPM 138 920
Berlin December 1975	BPO	DG 2530 884 DG 415 979-2

Symphony in C

Berlin April 1970	BPO	DG 2530 267

Symphony of Psalms

Berlin December 1977	BPO Chorus of Deutsche Oper	DG 2531 048

Suppé

The Beautiful Galathea, Overture

Berlin September 1968	BPO	DG 2530 051
		DG 2543 533

Jolly Robbers, Overture

Berlin September 1969	BPO	DG 2530 051
		DG 2543 533

Light Cavalry, Overture

London July 1955	Philharmonia	Columbia 33CX 1335
		Toshiba EAC 37020-38*
London September 1960	Philharmonia	Columbia 33CX 1758
		Columbia SAX 2404
		World Records ST 838
		EMI SLS 839*
		EMI CFP 40368
Berlin September 1969	BPO	DG 2530 051
		DG 2535 310
		DG 2535 629
		DG 2543 533
		DG 415 377-2

Morning, Noon and Night in Vienna, Overture

Berlin September 1969	BPO	DG 2530 051
		DG 415 377-2

Pique Dame, Overture

Berlin September 1969	BPO	DG 2530 051
		DG 2535 629

Poet and Peasant, Overture

Berlin September 1969	BPO	DG 2530 051
		DG 2535 629
		DG 2543 533
		DG 415 377-2

You, My Austria, March (arr. Doblinger)

Berlin March 1973	BPO Wind & Brass Ensemble	DG 2721 077

Tchaikovsky

Symphony No 1 "Winter Dreams"

Berlin January and February 1979	BPO	DG 2740 219* DG 2531 284 DG 415 024-1* DG 419 176-2

Symphony No 2 "Little Russian"

Berlin January and February 1979	BPO	DG 2740 219* DG 2531 285 DG 415 024-1* DG 419 177-2

Symphony No 3 "Polish"

Berlin January and February 1979	BPO	DG 2740 219* DG 2531 286 DG 415 024-1* DG 419 178-2

Symphony No 4

London July 1953	Philharmonia	Columbia 33CX 1139 Toshiba EAC 37020-38*
Berlin February and March 1960	BPO	Columbia 33CX 1704 Columbia SAX 2357 World Records ST 872 EMI SXLP 30433
Berlin October 1966	BPO	DG SKL 922-928* DG 139 017 DG 2740 126*
Berlin September 1971	BPO	EMI SLS 833* EMI ASD 2814
Berlin December 1976	BPO	DG 2530 883 DG 2740 219*
Vienna September 1984	VPO	DG 415 348-1 DG 415 348-2

Symphony No 5

May and July 1952 and June 1953	Philharmonia	Columbia 33CX 1133 Toshiba EAC 37020-38*
Turin March 1953	RAI Turin Orchestra	Fonit Cetra LAR 46*
Berlin September 1965	BPO	DG SKL 922-928* DG 139 018 DG 2542 108 DG 2740 126*
Berlin September 1971	BPO	EMI SLS 833* EMI ASD 2815
Berlin October 1975	BPO	DG 2530 699 DG 2740 219* DG 419 066-1
Vienna March 1984	VPO	DG 415 094-1 <u>DG 415 094-2</u>

Symphony No 6 "Pathétique"

Berlin 1939	BPO	Polydor 67499/500/501/ 502/503/504 Top Classic TC 9055
Vienna November 1948 and January 1949	VPO	Columbia LX 1234/5/6/7/8/9 (Auto LX 8699/700/1/2/3/4) Columbia 33CX 1026 Toshiba EAC 30105
London May 1955 and June 1956	Philharmonia	Columbia 33CX 1377 EMI SXLP 30534
Berlin February 1964	BPO	DG LPM 18 921/SLPM 138 921 DG SKL 922-928* DG 2740 126*
Berlin September 1971	BPO	EMI SLS 833* EMI ASD 2816
Berlin January 1976	BPO	DG 2530 774 DG 2740 219* DG 419 486-1
Vienna January 1984	VPO	DG 415 095-1 <u>DG 415 095-2</u>

Piano Concerto No 1

Vienna September 1962	Vienna Symphony Richter	DG LPM 18 822/SLPM 138 822 DG SKL 922-928* DG 2740 126* DG 419 068-1 DG 419 068-2
Paris February 1970	Orchestre de Paris Weisssenberg	EMI ASD 2576
Berlin November 1975	BPO Berman	DG 2530 677 DG 410 978-1

Violin Concerto

Berlin November 1965	BPO Ferras	DG SKL 922-928* DG 139 028 DG 2740 126* DG 2740 137* DG 2543 529

Variations on a Rococo theme

Berlin September 1968	BPO Rostropovich	DG 139 044 DG 2740 126* DG 413 819-2

Serenade for Strings

Berlin October 1966	BPO	DG SKL 922-928* DG 139 060 DG 2740 126* DG 415 855-1
Berlin September 1980	BPO	DG 2532 012 DG 400 038-2

1812 Overture

London January 1958	Philharmonia	Columbia 33CX 1571 Columbia SAX 2302 EMI SLS 839* EMI SXDW 3048*
Berlin October 1966	BPO Serge Jaroff's Don Cossack Choir	DG SKL 922-928* DG 139 029 DG 2538 142 DG 2740 126* DG 2543 532 DG 415 855-1 DG 419 177-2

Capriccio Italien

Berlin October 1966	BPO	DG SKL 922-928* DG 139 028 DG 2543 529 DG 419 178-2

Polonaise and Waltz (Eugene Onegin)
=====

Berlin December 1970   BPO   DG 2530 200
                                            DG 415 855-1
                                            DG 419 176-2

Marche slave
=====

Berlin October 1966   BPO   DG SKL 922-928*
                                            DG 139 029
                                            DG 2740 126*
                                            DG 2543 532
                                            DG 419 066-1
                                            DG 419 176-2

Romeo and Juliet, Fantasy Overture
=====

Vienna October 1946   VPO   Columbia LX 1033/4/5
                                            (Auto LX 8583/4/5)
                                            Toshiba EAC 30112

Vienna March 1960   VPO   Decca LXT 5629/SXL 2269
                                            Decca SPA 119
                                            Decca 417 722-2

Berlin October 1966   BPO   DG SKL 922-928*
                                            DG 139 029
                                            DG 2740 126*
                                            DG 2725 105*
                                            DG 2543 532
                                            DG 419 481-1

Berlin September 1982   BPO   DG 2561 408
                                            DG 410 873-1
                                            DG 410 873-2

The Nutcracker, Ballet Suite
=====

London July and   Philharmonia   Columbia LX 1599 & 1602
December 1952   (excerpts only)
                                            Columbia 33CX 1033
                                            Toshiba EAC 37020-38*

Vienna September 1961   VPO   Decca LXT 5673/SXL 2308
                                            Decca JB 16
                                            Decca 417 274-1
                                            Decca 417 700-2

Berlin October 1966   BPO   DG SKL 922-928*
                                            DG 139 030
                                            DG 2740 126*
                                            DG 2725 105*
                                            DG 419 175-2
                                            DG 419 481-1

Berlin September 1982   BPO   DG 2561 408
                                            DG 410 873-1
                                            DG 410 873-2

The Sleeping Beauty, Ballet Suite

London November and December 1952	Philharmonia	Columbia 33CX 1065 Toshiba EAC 37020-38*
London January 1959	Philharmonia	Columbia SAX 2306 EMI SLS 839* EMI SXLP 30200 Longanesi Periodici CGL 16 EMI EMX 41 22067-1
Vienna March 1965	VPO	Decca LXT 6187/SXL 6187 Decca JB 35 Decca 417 274-1 Decca 417 700-2
Berlin January and February 1971	BPO	DG 2530 195 DG 2725 105* DG 419 175-2 DG 419 481-1

Swan Lake, Ballet Suite

London November and December 1952	Philharmonia	Columbia 33CX 1065 Toshiba EAC 37020-38*
London January 1959	Philharmonia	Columbia SAX 2306 EMI SLS 839* EMI SXLP 30200 Longanesi Periodici CGL 16 EMI EMX 41 22067-1
Vienna March 1965	VPO	Decca LXT 6187/SXL 6187 Decca JB 35 Decca 417 274-1 Decca 417 700-2
Berlin January and February 1971	BPO	DG 2530 195 DG 2725 105* DG 419 175-2

Teike

Old Comrades, March

Berlin March 1973	BPO Wind & Brass Ensemble	DG 2721 077* DG 2535 647 DG 2535 686

Telemann

Trumpet Concerto in D (ed. Grebe)

Berlin May 1974	BPO André	EMI ASD 3044

Torelli

Concerto Op 8 No 6 "Christmas Concerto"

St Moritz August 1970	BPO	DG 2530 070 DG 2542 123 DG 415 027-1* DG 419 413-1

Vaughan Williams

Fantasia on a Theme by Thomas Tallis

London November 1953	Philharmonia	Columbia 33CX 1159 Toshiba EAC 37020-38* EMI XLP 60002

Verdi

Aida

Vienna September 1959	VPO Vienna Singverein Tebaldi, Simionato, Ratti, Bergonzi, MacNeil, Corena, Van Mill, Di Palma	Decca LXT 5539/40/41 Decca SXL 2167/8/9 Decca 414 087-1 Excerpts: Decca LXT 5597/SXL 2242
Vienna May 1979	VPO Vienna State Opera Chorus Freni, Baltsa, Ricciarelli, Carreras, Cappuccilli, R.Raimondi, T.Moser, Van Dam	EMI SLS 5205 EMI EX 29 0808-3

Aida, Prelude

Berlin September 1975	BPO	DG 2707 090* DG 413 544-1*

Dance of the Priestesses, Dance of the Moorish Slaves and Act 2 Ballet Music (Aida)

Berlin December 1970	BPO	DG 2530 200 DG 415 856-1 DG 415 855-2

Ballet Music, Act 2 (Aida)

London November 1954	Philharmonia	Columbia 33CX 1327 Toshiba EAC 37020-38*
London September 1960	Philharmonia	Columbia 33CX 1774 Columbia SAX 2421

Alzira, Overture

Berlin September 1975   BPO   DG 2707 090*
                                                     DG 413 544-1*

Aroldo, Overture

Berlin September 1975   BPO   DG 2707 090*
                                                     DG 413 544-1*

Attila, Prelude

Berlin September 1975   BPO   DG 2707 090*
                                                     DG 413 544-1*

Un Ballo in Maschera, Prelude

Berlin September 1975   BPO   DG 2707 090*
                                                     DG 413 544-1*
                                                     DG 419 622-2

La Battaglia di Legnano, Overture

Berlin September 1975   BPO   DG 2707 090*
                                                     DG 413 544-1*
                                                     DG 419 622-2

Il Corsaro, Overture

Berlin September 1975   BPO   DG 2707 090*
                                                     DG 413 544-1*
                                                     DG 419 622-2

Don Carlo

Salzburg July 1958   VPO   Historical Operatic
(Live)   Vienna State Opera Chorus   Treasures ERR 119
                                  Jurinac, Simionato,   Fonit Cetra LO 72
                                  Rothenberger, Balatsch,   Foyer FO 1029
                                  Fernandi, Siepi,   Excerpts:
                                  Bastianini, Stefanoni,   Longanesi Periodici GML 19
                                  C.Schmidt, Foster, Zaccaria

Berlin September 1978   BPO   EMI SLS 5154
                                  Chorus of Deutsche Oper
                                  Freni, Baltsa, Gruberova,
                                  Hendricks, Carreras,
                                  Nitsche, Cappuccilli,
                                  Van Dam, Ghiaurov,
                                  R.Raimondi, Meletti, Lang,
                                  Banuelas, Becker, Röhrl,
                                  Grönroos, Sardi

Ella giammai m'amò (Don Carlo)

| London November 1949 | Philharmonia
Christoff | HMV DB 21007
EMI 1C 147 03336/7M*
EMI RLS 735* |

Ernani, Prelude

| Berlin September 1975 | BPO | DG 2707 090*
DG 413 544-1*
DG 419 622-2 |

Falstaff

| London June 1956 | Philharmonia
Chorus
Schwarzkopf, Moffo,
Merriman, Barbieri, Alva,
Gobbi, Panerai, Zaccaria,
Spataro, Ercolani | Columbia 33CX 1410/11/12
Columbia SAX 2254/5/6
EMI SLS 5037
EMI SLS 5211
Excerpts:
Columbia 33CX 1939
Columbia SAX 2578 |
| Vienna May 1980 | VPO
Vienna State Opera Chorus
Kabaivanska, Perry,
T.Schmidt, C.Ludwig,
Araiza, Taddei, Panerai,
Di Palma, Zednik, Davià | Philips 6769 060
Philips 412 263-2
Excerpts: Philips 411 423-1
Philips 411 423-2 |

La Forza del Destino, Overture

| Berlin 1939 | Berlin Staatskapelle | Polydor 67466 |
| Berlin February 1975 | BPO | DG 2707 090*
DG 413 544-1*
DG 419 622-2 |

Un Giorgno di Regno, Overture

| Berlin September 1975 | BPO | DG 2707 090*
DG 413 544-1* |

Giovanna d'Arco, Overture

| Berlin September 1975 | BPO | DG 2707 090*
DG 413 544-1* |

Luisa Miller, Overture

| Berlin September 1975 | BPO | DG 2707 090*
DG 413 544-1*
DG 419 622-2 |

Macbeth, Prelude

Berlin September 1975   BPO   DG 2707 090*
                                             DG 413 544-1*
                                             DG 419 622-2

I Masnadieri, Prelude

Berlin September 1975   BPO   DG 2707 090*
                                             DG 413 544-1*
                                             DG 419 622-2

Nabucco, Overture

Berlin September 1975   BPO   DG 2707 090*
                                             DG 413 544-1*
                                             DG 419 622-2

Oberto, Overture

Berlin September 1975   BPO   DG 2707 090*
                                             DG 413 544-1*

Otello

Vienna May 1961   VPO   Decca MET 209/10/11
                      Vienna State Opera Chorus   Decca SET 209/10/11
                      Concert Association of the   Decca D55 D3
                      Vienna State Opera Chorus   Decca 411 618-2
                      Vienna Childrens' Choir   Excerpts:
                      Tebaldi, Satre, Del Monaco,   Decca LXT 5863/SXL 2314
                      Romanato, Protti, Corena,
                      Krause, Cesarini, Arbace   EMI SLS 975

Berlin April and May 1973   BPO
                      Chorus of Deutsche Oper
                      Freni, Malagù, Vickers,
                      Bottion, Sénéchal, Glossop,
                      Van Dam, Machi, Helm

Ballet Music (Otello)

Berlin December 1970   BPO   DG 2530 200

Rigoletto, Prelude

Berlin September 1975   BPO   DG 2707 090*
                                             DG 413 544-1*
                                             DG 419 622-2

La Traviata

Milan December 1964 (Live)	La Scala Orchestra and Chorus Freni, Righetti, Leoni, Cioni, Sereni, Goretti, Giacomotti, Maionica, Zaccaria, Ricciardi, Carbonari, Forti	Paragon PCD 84006/7

La Traviata, Act 1 Prelude

Turin 1942	EIAR Turin Orchestra	Polydor 68156
Berlin September 1975	BPO	DG 2707 090* DG 413 544-1* DG 419 622-2

La Traviata, Act 3 Prelude

Turin 1942	EIAR Turin Orchestra	Polydor 68156
London July 1954	Philharmonia	Columbia 33CX 1265 Toshiba EAC 37020-38*
London January 1959	Philharmonia	Columbia SAX 2294 EMI SLS 5019*
Berlin September 1967	BPO	DG 139 031 DG 419 257-2*

Il Trovatore

Milan August 1956	La Scala Orchestra and Chorus Callas, Barbieri, Villa, Di Stefano, Panerai, Zaccaria, Ercolani, Mauri	Columbia 33CX 1483/4/5 EMI SLS 869 Excerpts: Columbia 33CX 1682
Salzburg July 1962 (Live)	VPO Vienna State Opera Chorus Price, Simionato, Dutoit, Corelli, Bastianini, Frese, Zaccaria, Equiluz, Zimmer	Morgan Records MOR 6201 HRE Records HRE 287 Fonit Cetra ARK 7 Movimento Musica 03.018 Melodram MEL 710 Movimento Musica 012.001 Rodolphe RPC 32482/3
Berlin September 1977	BPO Chorus of Deutsche Oper Price, Obraztsova, Venuti, Bonisolli, Cappuccilli, R.Raimondi, Nitsche, Engel	EMI SLS 5111 EMI EX 29 09533

I Vespri Siciliani, Overture

Berlin September 1975	BPO	DG 2707 090* DG 413 544-1* DG 419 622-2

Requiem Mass

Salzburg August 1949 (Live)	VPO Vienna Singverein Zadek, Klose, Rosvaenge, Christoff	Discocorp RR 361 Rodolphe RP 12403/4
Moscow September 1964 (Live)	La Scala Orchestra and Chorus Price, Cossotto, Bergonzi, Ghiaurov	Melodiya M10 45785005 Foyer FO 1045
Berlin January 1972	BPO Vienna Singverein Freni, C.Ludwig, Cossutta, Ghiaurov	DG 2707 065 DG 413 215-1
Vienna January 1984	VPO Concert Association of Vienna State Opera Chorus Sofia National Opera Chorus Tomowa-Sintow, Baltsa, Carreras, Van Dam	DG 415 091-1 DG 415 091-2

Vivaldi

The Four Seasons

St Moritz August 1972	BPO Schwalbé	DG 2530 296 DG 415 201-1 DG 415 301-2 DG 419 488-1
Vienna January 1984	VPO Mutter	EMI EL 27 0102-1 EMI CDC 747043-2

Sinfonia in B minor "Al Santo Sepolcro"

St Moritz August 1970	BPO	DG 2530 094 DG 415 027-1*

Concerto for Strings in G "Alla Rustica"

St Moritz August 1970	BPO	DG 2530 094 DG 415 027-1* DG 419 046-1

Concerto for Strings in D minor "Madrigalesco"

St Moritz August 1970	BPO	DG 2530 094 DG 415 027-1* DG 419 046-2

Flute Concerto in G minor "La Notte"

Berlin September 1983	BPO Blau	DG 413 309-1 DG 413 309-2

Violin Concerto in E "L'Amoroso"

St Moritz August 1970	BPO Brandis	DG 2530 094 DG 415 027-1* DG 419 046-1 DG 419 046-2

Violin Concerto in D "L'Inquietudine"

St Moritz August 1970	BPO Brandis	DG 2530 094 DG 415 027-1*

Double Violin Concerto in A minor

St Moritz August 1970	BPO Brandis Maas	DG 2530 094 DG 415 027-1*

J. F. Wagner

Tirolean Woodcutter Lads, March (arr. Tanzer)

Berlin March 1973	BPO Wind & Brass Ensemble	DG 2721 077*

Under the Double Eagle, March (arr. Mosheimer)

Berlin March 1973	BPO Wind & Brass Ensemble	DG 2721 077* DG 2535 647

Wagner

Der fliegende Holländer

Berlin December 1981 and September 1983 and Salzburg March 1982	BPO Concert Association of the Vienna State Opera Chorus Vejzovic, Borris, Van Dam, Moll, Hofmann, T.Moser	EMI EX 27 0013-3 EMI CDS 747 054-8

Der fliegende Holländer, Overture

Berlin September 1960	BPO	Columbia 33CX 1791 Columbia SAX 2439 World Records ST 639 EMI SXLP 30210 EMI 1C 137 54360/1/2/3* EMI EMX 41 2052-1
Berlin September and October 1974	BPO	EMI ASD 3160 EMI SXLP 30506 EMI EG 29 0411-1

Spinning Chorus (Der fliegende Holländer)

Vienna November 1948	VPO Vienna State Opera Chorus Schuster	Columbia LX 1440 Toshiba EAC 30109

Introduction Act 3 and Sailors' Chorus (Der fliegende Holländer)

Vienna November 1949	VPO Vienna State Opera Chorus	Columbia LX 1440 Toshiba EAC 30109

Götterdämmerung

Bayreuth August 1951 (Live)	Bayreuth Festival Orchestra Bayreuth Festival Chorus Varnay, Mödl, Töpper, Schwarzkopf, H.Ludwig, Siewert, Malaniuk, Aldenhoff, Uhde, Pflanzl, Weber	Columbia unpublished
Berlin October 1969	BPO Chorus of Deutsche Oper Dernesch, Janowitz, C.Ludwig, Ligendza, Rebmann, E.Moser, Reynolds, Chookasian, Brilioth, Kelemen, Stewart, Ridderbusch	DG 2720 019 DG 2716 001 DG 2720 051* DG 2740 148 DG 2740 240* DG 415 155-2 Excerpts: DG 2535 239 DG 415 256-2

Lohengrin

Berlin December 1975, March 1976 and May 1981	BPO Chorus of Deutsche Oper Tomowa-Sintow, Vejzovic, Kollo, Nimsgern, Kerns, Ridderbusch, Lang, Maus, Vantin, Becker	EMI SLS 5237

Lohengrin, Act 1 Prelude

Berlin September 1960	BPO	Columbia 33CX 1791 Columbia SAX 2439 World Records ST 639 EMI SXLP 30210 EMI 1C 137 54360/1/2/3 EMI EMX 41 2052-1
Berlin September and October 1974	BPO	EMI ASD 3130

Lohengrin, Act 3 Prelude

Vienna November 1949	VPO	Columbia LX 1360 Toshiba EAC 30109
Berlin September and October 1974	BPO	EMI ASD 3160

Bridal Chorus (Lohengrin)

Vienna November 1948	VPO Vienna State Opera Chorus	Columbia unpublished
Vienna November 1949	VPO Vienna State Opera Chorus	Columbia LX 1360 Toshiba EAC 30109

Die Meistersinger von Nürnberg

Bayreuth July and August 1951 (Live)	Bayreuth Festival Orchestra Bayreuth Festival Chorus Schwarzkopf, Malaniuk, Hopf, Edelmann, Kunz, Dalberg, Majkut, Berg, Pflanzl, Janko, Mikorey, Stolze, Tandler, Borst, Van Mill, Unger, Faulhaber	Columbia LX 1465-1498 (Auto LX 8851-8884) Columbia 33CX 1021/2/3/4/5 EMI RLS 7708 EMI 143 3903
Dresden November and December 1970	Dresden Staatskapelle Leipzig Radio Chorus Dresden State Opera Chorus Donath, Hesse, Kollo, Adam, Ridderbusch, Evans, Büchner, Lunow, Kelemen, Rotzsch, Bindszus, Reeh, Hiestermann, Polster, Vogel, Schreier, Moll	EMI SLS 957

Die Meistersinger von Nürnberg, Act 1 Prelude

Berlin 1939	Berlin Staatskapelle	Polydor 67532
Berlin February 1957	BPO	Columbia 33CX 1496 EMI 1C 137 54360/1/2/3*
Berlin September and October 1974	BPO	EMI ASD 3160 EMI EG 29 0411-1 Toshiba CC28-99009 EMI CDM 769 0192
Berlin February 1984	BPO	DG 413 754-1 DG 413 754-2

Die Meistersinger von Nürnberg, Act 3 Prelude

Berlin 1939	Berlin Staatskapelle	Polydor 67527
Berlin February 1984	BPO	DG 413 754-1 DG 413 754-2

Da zu dir der Heiland kam (Die Meistersinger von Nürnberg)

Vienna November 1949	VPO Vienna State Opera Chorus	Columbia LX 1258 Toshiba EAC 30109

Wach auf ! (Die Meistersinger von Nürnberg)

Vienna November 1949	VPO Vienna State Opera Chorus	Columbia LX 1258 Toshiba EAC 20109

Flieder-Monolog (Die Meistersinger von Nürnberg)

Vienna October 1946	VPO Hotter	Columbia unpublished

Wahn-Monolog (Die Meistersinger von Nürnberg)

Vienna October 1946	VPO Hotter	Columbia unpublished

Parsifal

Berlin December 1979 and January and July 1980	BPO Chorus of Deutsche Oper Vejzovic, Hofmann, Moll, Van Dam, Nimsgern, Halem, Schwarz, Lambriks, Perry, Gjevang, Hendricks, Soffel, Nielsen, Michael. Yachmi, Ahnsjö, Rydl, Hopfner, Tichy	DG 2741 002 DG 413 347-2 Excerpts: DG 2532 033

Parsifal, Act 1 Prelude

Berlin September and October 1974	BPO	EMI ASD 3160 EMI SLS 5086*

Parsifal, Act 3 Prelude

Berlin September and October 1974	BPO	EMI ASD 3160

Das Rheingold

Bayreuth August 1951 (Live)	Bayreuth Festival Orchestra Malaniuk, Brivkalne, Siewert, Schwarzkopf, Wissman, Töpper, Björling, Kuen, Fritz, Windgassen, Faulhaber, Weber, Dalberg, Pflanzl	Melodram MEL 516
Berlin December 1967 and January 1968	BPO Veasey, Mangelsdorff, Dominguez, Donath, E.Moser, Reynolds, Fischer-Dieskau, Grobe, Stolze, Wohlfahrt, Kelemen, Kerns, Talvela, Ridderbusch	DG SKL 104 966/7/8 DG 2709 023 DG 2720 051* DG 2740 145 DG 2740 240* DG 415 141-2 Excerpts: DG 136 437 DG 2535 239 DG 415 256-2

Siegfried

Bayreuth August 1951 (Live)	Bayreuth Festival Orchestra Varnay, Lipp, Siewert, Aldenhoff, Kuen, Björling, Pflanzl, Dalberg	Foyer FO 1004 Excerpt (Forest Murmurs): Foyer FO 1034*
Berlin December 1968	BPO Dernesch, Gayer, Dominguez, Thomas, Stolze, Stewart, Kelemen, Ridderbusch	DG 643 536/7/8/9/40 DG 2713 003 DG 2720 051* DG 2740 147 DG 2740 240* DG 415 150-2 Excerpts: DG 2535 239 DG 415 256-2

Heda ! Du Fauler ! Bist du nun fertig....to end Act 1 (Siegfried)

Vienna April 1962 (Live)	VPO Beirer, Klein	Melodram MEL 427*

Tannhäuser

Vienna January 1963 (Live)	VPO Vienna State Opera Chorus Brouwenstijn, Janowitz, C.Ludwig, Beirer, Frick, Wächter, Kmennt, Welter, Equiluz, Franc	Melodram MEL 427 Nuova Era 013.6307/8/9

Tannhäuser, Overture (original version)

Berlin January 1957	BPO	Columbia 33CX 1496 EMI 1C 137 54360/1/2/3*
Berlin February 1984	BPO	DG 413 754-1 DG 413 754-2

Tannhäuser, Overture and Venusberg Music (Paris version)

Berlin September and October 1974	BPO Chorus of Deutsche Oper	EMI ASD 3130 EMI EG 29 0411-1 <u>Toshiba CC28-99009</u> <u>EMI CDM 769 0192</u>

Venusberg Music (Tannhäuser)

London November 1954	Philharmonia	Columbia 33CX 1335 Toshiba EAC 37020-38*
London September 1960	Philharmonia	Columbia 33CX 1774 Columbia SAX 2421
Berlin February 1984	BPO	DG 413 754-1 <u>DG 413 754-2</u>

March and Entry of the Guests (Tannhäuser)

Vienna November 1949	VPO Vienna State Opera Chorus	Columbia LX 1347 Toshiba EAC 30109

Tristan und Isolde

Bayreuth July 1952 (Live)	Bayreuth Festival Orchestra Bayreuth Festival Chorus Mödl, Malaniuk, Vinay, Hotter, Weber, Stolze, Uhde, Faulhaber, Unger	Fonit Cetra LO 47 Melodram MEL 525 Foyer FO 1038 <u>Hunt Productions HUNTCD 528</u> Excerpts: Rodolphe RP 12704 Maestri del Secolo APE 1210 WG Records WG 30010 Foyer FO 1034*
Berlin December 1971 and January 1972	BPO Chorus of Deutsche Oper Dernesch, C.Ludwig, Vickers, Berry, Weikl, Ridderbusch, Schreier, Vantin	EMI SLS 963 <u>Excerpts:</u> EMI ASD 3354

Tristan und Isolde, Prelude and Liebestod

Berlin January 1957	BPO	Columbia 33CX 1496 EMI 1C 137 54360/1/2/3*
Berlin September and October 1974	BPO	EMI ASD 3130 EMI EG 29 0411-1 <u>Toshiba CC28-99009</u> <u>EMI CDM 769 0192</u>
Berlin February 1984	BPO	DG 413 754-1 <u>DG 413 754-2</u>

Die Walküre

Bayreuth August 1951 (Live)	Bayreuth Festival Orchestra Varnay, Rysanek, H.Ludwig, Treptow, Van Mill, Björling, Friedland, Wild, Thomamüller, Lausch, Siewert, Töpper, Malaniuk	Acts 1 and 2: Columbia unpublished Act 3: Columbia LX 1447-1454 (Auto LX 8835-8842) Columbia 33CX 1005/S EMI 1C 181 03035/6M Toshiba EAC 60215/S
Berlin September 1966	BPO Crespin, Janowitz, Veasey, Vickers, Talvela, Stewart, Rebmann, Steger, Ahlin, Mastilovic, Ordassy, Brockhaus, Ericson, Jenckel	DG LPM 39 229/30/31/32/33 DG SLPM 139 229/30/31/32/33 DG 2713 002 DG 2720 051* DG 2740 146 DG 2740 240* DG 415 145-2 Excerpts: DG 136 435 DG 2535 239 DG 415 256-2

Siegfried Idyll

Berlin February 1977	BPO	DG 2707 102* DG 2543 510 DG 419 196-2*

Wagnes

The Bosnians are coming, March

Berlin March 1973	BPO Wind & Brass Ensemble	DG 2721 077*

Waldteufel

The Skaters' Waltz

London July 1953	Philharmonia	Columbia 33CX 1335 Toshiba EAC 37020-38*
London September 1960	Philharmonia	Columbia 33CX 1758 Columbia SAX 2404 World Records ST 838 EMI SLS 839* EMI SXLP 30224 EMI SXDW 3048* EMI CFP 40368

Weber

Abu Hassan, Overture

Berlin February 1972	BPO	DG 2530 315 DG 419 070-1 DG 419 070-2

Euryanthe, Overture

Berlin February 1972	BPO	DG 2530 315 DG 419 070-1 DG 419 070-2

Der Freischütz, Overture

Amsterdam 1943	Concertgebouw	Polydor 68354/5
Berlin September 1960	BPO	Columbia 33CX 1791 Columbia SAX 2439 World Records ST 639 EMI SXLP 30210 EMI EMX 41 2052-1
Berlin January and February 1971	BPO	DG 2530 315 DG 419 070-1 DG 419 070-2
Berlin January 1981	BPO	EMI ASD 4072 Toshiba CC28-99008 EMI CDM 769 0202

Oberon, Overture

Berlin January and February 1971	BPO	DG 2530 315 DG 2535 310 DG 419 070-1 DG 419 070-2

Peter Schmoll, Overture

Berlin February 1972	BPO	DG 2530 315 DG 419 070-1 DG 419 070-2

Ruler of the Spirits, Overture

Berlin February 1972	BPO	DG 2530 315 DG 419 070-1 DG 419 070-2

Invitation to the Dance (orch. Berlioz)

London January 1958	Philharmonia	Columbia 33CX 1571 Columbia SAX 2302 EMI SLS 5019*
Berlin September 1971	BPO	DG 2530 244 DG 419 070-1 DG 419 070-2
Berlin December 1983	BPO	DG 413 587-1 DG 413 587-2

Webern

Five Movements op 5

| Berlin November and December 1973 | BPO | DG 2711 014* |
| | | DG 2530 488 |

Passacaglia op 1

| Berlin February 1974 | BPO | DG 2711 014* |
| | | DG 2530 488 |

Six Pieces for Orchestra op 6

| Berlin November and December 1973 | BPO | DG 2711 014* |
| | | DG 2530 488 |

Symphony op 21

| Berlin February 1974 | BPO | DG 2711 014* |
| | | DG 2530 488 |

Weinberger

Schwanda the Bagpiper, Polka

| London July 1954 | Philharmonia | Columbia 33CX 1335 |
| | | Toshiba EAC 37020-38* |

London September 1960	Philharmonia	Columbia 33CX 1758
		Columbia SAX 2404
		World Records ST 838
		EMI SLS 5019*
		EMI CFP 40368

Willis

It came upon the Midnight clear

Vienna June 1961	VPO	Decca LXT 5657/SXL 2294
	Vienna Singverein	Decca JB 38
	Price	

Wolf-Ferrari

The Jewels of the Madonna, Act 3 Intermezzo

| Berlin September 1967 | BPO | DG 139 031 |
| | | DG 419 257-2* |

Traditional & Anonymous

<u>Traditional Christmas Songs: Angels we have heard on high (Gloria in excelsis Deo);
O Tannenbaum; God rest ye Merry Gentlemen</u>

Vienna June 1961	VPO Vienna Singverein Price	Decca LXT 5657/SXL 2294 Decca JB 38

<u>Anonymous Marches: Finnish Cavalry March; Coburg March; The Entry into Paris;
Pappenheim March; St Petersburg March</u>

Berlin March 1973	BPO Wind & Brass Ensemble	DG 2721 077* DG 2535 647 (St Petersburg March & Entry into Paris only) DG 2535 686 (St Petersburg March only)

<u>National Anthems of the 17 Member States of the Council of Europe (composers not
credited)</u>: Austria; Belgium; Cyprus; Denmark; West Germany; France; Iceland;
Ireland; Italy; Luxemburg; Malta; Netherlands; Norway; Sweden; Switzerland;
Turkey; Great Britain

Berlin February and March 1972	BPO	DG 2530 250

Appendix A:
Index of Artists who have performed in recordings under Karajan's direction

Orchestras

Berlin Philharmonic
Berlin Philharmonic Wind and Brass Ensembles
Berlin Staatskapelle
Bayreuth Festival Orchestra
Cologne Radio Orchestra
Concertgebouw Orchestra Amsterdam
Dresden Staatskapelle
EIAR Turin Orchestra
La Scala Orchestra Milan
Lucerne Festival Orchestra
Orchestre de Paris
Philharmonia Orchestra
RAI Rome Orchestra
RAI Turin Orchestra
RIAS Orchestra Berlin
Vienna Philharmonic
Vienna Symphony Orchestra

Choirs

Bancroft's School Choir
Bayreuth Festival Chorus
Berlin Cathedral Choir
Chorus of Deutsche Oper Berlin
Chorus of La Scala Milan
Cologne Radio Chorus
Dresden State Opera Chorus
Concert Association of the Vienna State Opera Chorus
Leipzig Radio Chorus
Loughton High School Choir
Paris Opera Chorus
RAI Rome Chorus
RIAS Chamber Choir Berlin
Schöneberg Boys' Choir
Serge Jaroff's Don Cossack Choir
Sofia Radio Chorus
St Hedwig's Cathedral Choir Berlin
Tölz Boys Choir
Vienna Boys' Choir
Vienna Childrens' Choir
Vienna Männergesangverein
Vienna Singverein
Vienna State Opera Chorus

Instrumentalists

Anda, Geza
André, Maurice
Berman, Lazar
Blau, Andreas
Brain, Dennis
Brandis, Thomas
Braun, Manfred
Cherkassky, Shura
Cochereau, Pierre
Eschenbach, Christoph
Ferras, Christian
Fournier, Pierre
Galway, James
Gieseking, Walter
Hauptmann, Norbert
Helmis, Fritz
James, Cecil
Kempff, Wilhelm
Kremer, Gidon
Leimer, Kurt
Leister, Karl
Lipatti, Dinu
Ma, Yo Yo
Maas, Emil
Meneses, Antonio
Mutter, Anne-Sophie
Oistrakh, David
Parikian, Manoug
Piesk, Günther
Richter, Sviatoslav
Richter-Hasser, Hans
Rostropovich, Mstislav
Schwalbé, Michel
Seifert, Gerd
Spierer, Leon
Stähr, Herbert
Steins, Karl
Sutcliffe, Sidney
Walton, Bernard
Weissenberg, Alexis
Wlach, Leopold
Zeltser, Mark
Zimerman, Kristian
Zöller, Karlheinz

Sopranos

Adani, Mariella
Anderson, Sylvia

Barbaux, Christine
Battle, Kathleen
Behrens, Hildegard
Brivkalne, Paula
Brouwenstijn, Gré
Bünten, Wolfgang (boy sop.)

Callas, Maria
Carlyle, Joan
Carteri, Rosanna
Cebotari, Maria
Cotrubas, ILeana
Cuberli, Lella
Czeska, Hilde

Dernesch, Helga
Dobrianova, Najejda
Donath, Helen
Dörpinhans, Eleonore
Dutoit, Laurence

Felbermayer, Anni
Friedland, Brünnhild
Freni, Mirella

Gayer, Catherine
Gessendorf, Mechthild
Goltz, Christel
Griffel, Kay
Grosshans, Elke
Gruberova, Edita
Grümmer, Elisabeth
Güden, Hilde

Hallstein, Ingeborg
Harwood, Elizabeth
Hendricks, Barbara
Heigl, Martha
Hillebrecht, Hildegard
Hürdes, Evamaria

Janowitz, Gundula
Jenckel, Helga
Jurinac, Sena

Kabaiwanska, Raina
Konetzni, Hilde
Köth, Erika

Labruce, Evelyn
Lambriks, Marjon
Lausch, Eleanor
Leoni, Limbania
Ligendza, Catarina
Linval, Monique
Lipp, Wilma
Loose, Emmy
Lorand, Colette
Loulis, Glenys
Lövaas, Kari

Mangelsdorff, Simone
Marsh, Jane
Martinis, Carla
Martino, Adriana
Mastiloviv, Daniza
Mathis, Edith
Michael, Audrey
Miljakovic, Oliviera

Mödl, Martha
Moffo, Anna
Moser, Edda

Nielsen, Inga
Nilsson, Birgit

Ott, Catherine
Ott, Elfriede
Ott, Karin
Otto, Lisa

Perry, Janet
Pfülb, Tobias (boy sop.)
Plümacher, Hetty
Popp, Lucia
Poschner, Brigitte
Price, Leontyne
Pritchett, Carol

Rathauscher, Gisela
Ratti, Eugenia
Rebmann, Liselotte
Reinoso, Maria Teresa
Ricciarelli, Katia
Righetti, Romana
Rothenberger, Anneliese
Rysanek, Leonie

Schary, Elke
Scheyrer, Gerda
Schubert, Hedwig
Schulz, Christian (boy sop.)
Schwaiger, Rosl
Schwarzkopf, Elisabeth
Sciutti, Graziella
Seefried, Irmgard
Sima, Gabriele
Spiluttini, Gunda
Steger, Ingrid
Sterba, Rosl
Steinmassl, Hermine
Sterba, Rosl
Stich-Randall, Teresa
Stratas, Teresa
Streich, Rita
Stückl, Annelies

Tebaldi, Renata
Thomamüller, Lieselotte
Tomova-Sintow, Anna

Varnay, Astrid
Venuti, Maria
Villa, Luisa
Vishnevskaya, Galina

Welitsch, Ljuba
Weiss, Herbert (boy sop.)
Wild, Elfriede

Zadek, Hilde

Mezzo-sopranos and contraltos

Ahlin, Cvetka
Angervo, Helga
Allegri, Maria Gracia

Baltsa, Agnes
Barbieri, Fedora
Berbié, Jane
Borris, Kaja
Brockhaus, Lilo

Chookasian, Lili
Cossotto, Fiorenza
Cvejic, Biserka

Danieli, Lucia
Denize, Nadine
Dominguez, Oralia

Ericson, Barbro

Ferrier, Kathleen

Gjevang, Anne

Hellwig, Judith
Hesse, Ruth
Höffgen, Marga
Hoffman, Grace
Höngen, Elisabeth
Hintermeier, Margaretha

Ilosvay, Maria von

Killebrew, Gwendolyn
Klose, Margarete

Lilova, Margarita
Ludwig, Christa
Ludwig, Hanna

Macaux, Geneviève
Malagù, Stefania
Malaniuk, Ira
Merriman, Nan
Meyer, Kerstin
Mühlberger, Erna Maria
Müller-Molinari, Helga
Murray, Ann

Obraztsova, Elena

Radev, Marianne
Resnik, Regina
Reynolds, Anna
Ribacchi, Luisa
Rieger, Friedl
Rössl-Majdan, Hilde

Satre, Ana Raquel
Schmidt, Trudeliese
Schürhoff, Else
Schuster, Gertrud
Schwarz, Hanna
Siewert, Ruth
Simionato, Giulietta
Sjöstedt, Margarethe
Soffel, Doris
Stade, Frederica von
Stowasser, Magdalena

Töpper, Hertha
Veasey, Josephine
Vejzovic, Dunja

Watts, Helen

Yachmi, Rohangiz

Tenors

Ahnsjö, Claes
Aldenhoff, Bernd
Anheisser, Wolfgang
Araiza, Francisco
Arbace, Libero

Balatsch, Norbert
Banuelas, Roberto
Beirer, Hans
Benelli, Ugo
Bergonzi, Carlo
Besançon, Maurice
Bindzsus, Peter
Böhm, Karl-Walter
Bömches, Helge
Bonisolli, Franco
Bottion, Aldo
Brilioth, Helge
Büchner, Eberhard

Caron, Willi
Carmeli, Boris
Carreras, José
Christ, Rudolf
Cioni, Renato
Cole, Vinson
Corelli, Franco
Cossutta, Carlo
Cuenod, Hugues

Dermota, Anton
Diakov, Anton
Domingo, Placido

Equiluz, Kurt
Ercolani, Renato

Fernandi, Eugenio
Friedrich, Karl
Fritz, Walter

Gedda, Nicolai
Giacomotti, Alfredo
Gioretti, Giorgio
Grobe, Donald
Grönroos, Walton

Häfliger, Ernst
Heppe, Leo
Hiestermann, Horst
Hofmann, Peter
Hollweg, Werner
Holzherr, Wolfgang
Hopf, Hans
Hopfner, Heiner
Horn, Volker

Janko, Josef
Jokel, Hannes

King, James
Klein, Peter
Kmennt, Waldemar
Knutson, David
Koblitz, Ingo
Kollo, René
Krebs, Helmut
Kruse, Heinz
Krenn, Werner
Kuen, Paul

Laubenthal, Horst
Lorenzi, Ermanno
Ludwig, Walther

Majkut, Erich
Marinpouille, Michel
Maslennikov, Aleksei
Maus, Peter
Mikorey, Georg
Monaco, Mario del
Moser, Thomas

Nitsche, Horst

Ochman, Wieslaw

Patzak, Julius
Patzalt, Hermann
Pavarotti, Luciano
Pietsch, Gerhard
Pilard, Alain
Pirino, Antonio

Raimondi, Gianni
Reautschnigg, Johann
Renar, Karl
Romanato, Nello
Romani, Regolo
Rosvaenge, Helge
Rotzsch, Hans Joachim
Roux, Michel

Schock, Rudolf
Schooten, Frank
Schreier, Peter
Sénéchal, Michel
Simoneau, Leopold
Spataro, Tomaso
Sperlbauer, Fritz
Spiess, Ludovic
Stefano, Giuseppe di
Stolze, Gerhard

Thomas, Jess
Tomaschek, Adolf
Treptow, Günther

Unger, Gerhard

Valletti, Cesare
Vantin, Martin
Vickers, Jon
Vinay, Ramon

Winbergh, Gösta
Windgassen, Wolfgang
Witt, Josef
Wohlfahrt, Erwin
Wunderlich, Fritz

Zampieri, Giuseppe
Zednik, Heinz

Baritones and basses

Adam, Theo
Appelt, Hans Dieter

Badioli, Carlo
Bastianini, Ettore
Bastin, Jules
Becker, Josef
Benoit, Jean-Christophe
Berg, Hans
Berry, Walter
Bierbach, Franz

Björling, Sigurd
Böheim, Franz
Bömches, Helge
Borriello, Mario
Borst, Heinz
Boysen, Ralf
Bruscantini, Sesto
Burchuladze, Paata

Carbonari, Virgilio
Calabrese, Franco
Campi, Enrico
Cappuccilli, Piero
Cava, Carlo
Carlin, Mario
Cesarini, Athos
Christoff, Boris
Clabassi, Plinio
Corena, Fernando

Dalberg, Friedrich
Dam, José van
Davià, Federico
Demigny, Bernard
Dönch, Karl

Edelmann, Otto
Ellenbeck, Dieter
Engel, Martin
Evans, Geraint

Faulhaber, Werner
Felden, Wilhelm
Feller, Carlos
Fischer-Dieskau, Dietrich
Forti, Carlo
Foster, Norman
Franc, Tugomir
Frese, Siegfried Rudolf
Frick, Gottlob
Furlanetto, Ferruccio

Geisen, Erik
Ghiaurov, Nicolai
Glossop, Peter
Gobbi, Tito
Greindl, Josef
Guelfi, Giangiacomo
Guthrie, Frederick

Halem, Victor von
Häusler, Martin
Helm, Hans
Höfermayer, Walter
Hornik, Gottfried
Hotter, Hans

Karolidis, Paul
Kauffmann, Erich
Kelemen, Zoltan
Kerns, Robert
Knapp, Josef
Kraus, Otakar
Krause, Tom
Kreppel, Walter
Krukowski, Ernst
Kunz, Erich

Lang, Klaus
Lichtenberger, Hannes
London, George
Lunov, Horst
Luxon, Benjamin

Machi, Mario
MacNeil, Cornel
Maffeo, Gianni
Maionica, Silvio
Malta, Alexander
Mantovani, Dino
Markov, Sabin
Mariotti, Alfredo
Mauri, Giulio
Melbye, Mikael
Meletti, Carlo
Merrill, Robert
Metternich, Josef
Modesti, Giuseppe
Moll, Kurt
Monreale, Leonardo
Montarsolo, Paolo
Morresi, Giuseppe

Nessi, Giuseppe
Nicolai, Claudio
Nienstedt, Gerd

Ollendorff, Fritz

Palma, Piero de
Panerai, Rolando
Paskalis, Kostas
Pantscheff, Ljubomir
Panzenböck, Gerhard
Paunov, Milen
Petri, Mario
Pflanzl, Heinrich
Pernerstorfer, Alois
Pohl, Hans Dietrich
Polster, Hermann
Prey, Hermann
Prilcec, Zvonimir
Pröglhöf, Harald
Protti, Aldo

Quilico, Gino

Ramey, Samuel
Raimondi, Ruggiero
Reeh, Heinz
Rehfuss, Heinz
Ricciardi, Franco
Ridderbusch, Karl
Rintzler, Marius
Röhrl, Manfred
Rus, Marjan
Rydl, Kurt

Sardi, Ivan
Scheider, Wolfgang
Schmidt, Carlos
Schöffler, Paul
Schooten, Frank
Sereni, Mario
Siepi, Cesare
Signore, Gino del
Sordello, Enzo
Souzay, Gerard
Stefanoni, Mario
Stendoro, Giorgio
Stewart, Thomas
Stilwell, Richard
Strauss, Erich

Taddei, Giuseppe
Talvela, Martti
Tandler, Heinz
Terkal, Karl
Thomas, Pascal
Tichy, Georg

Uhde, Hermann
Uhl, Friedrich

Valenta, Leopold
Vinco, Ivo
Vogel, Siegfried

Wächter, Eberhard
Weber, Ludwig
Wegmann, Hans
Weikl, Bernd
Welter, Ludwig
Wiener, Otto
Wolfrum, Paul

Zeh, Walter
Zimmer, Rudolf

Speakers

Boysen, Rolf
Hirsch, Robert
Meinrad, Josef
Neugebauer, Alfred
Quadflieg, Will
Rothenberger, Anneliese
Schellow, Ernst
Schneider, Romy
Trümper, Helge
Ustinov, Peter

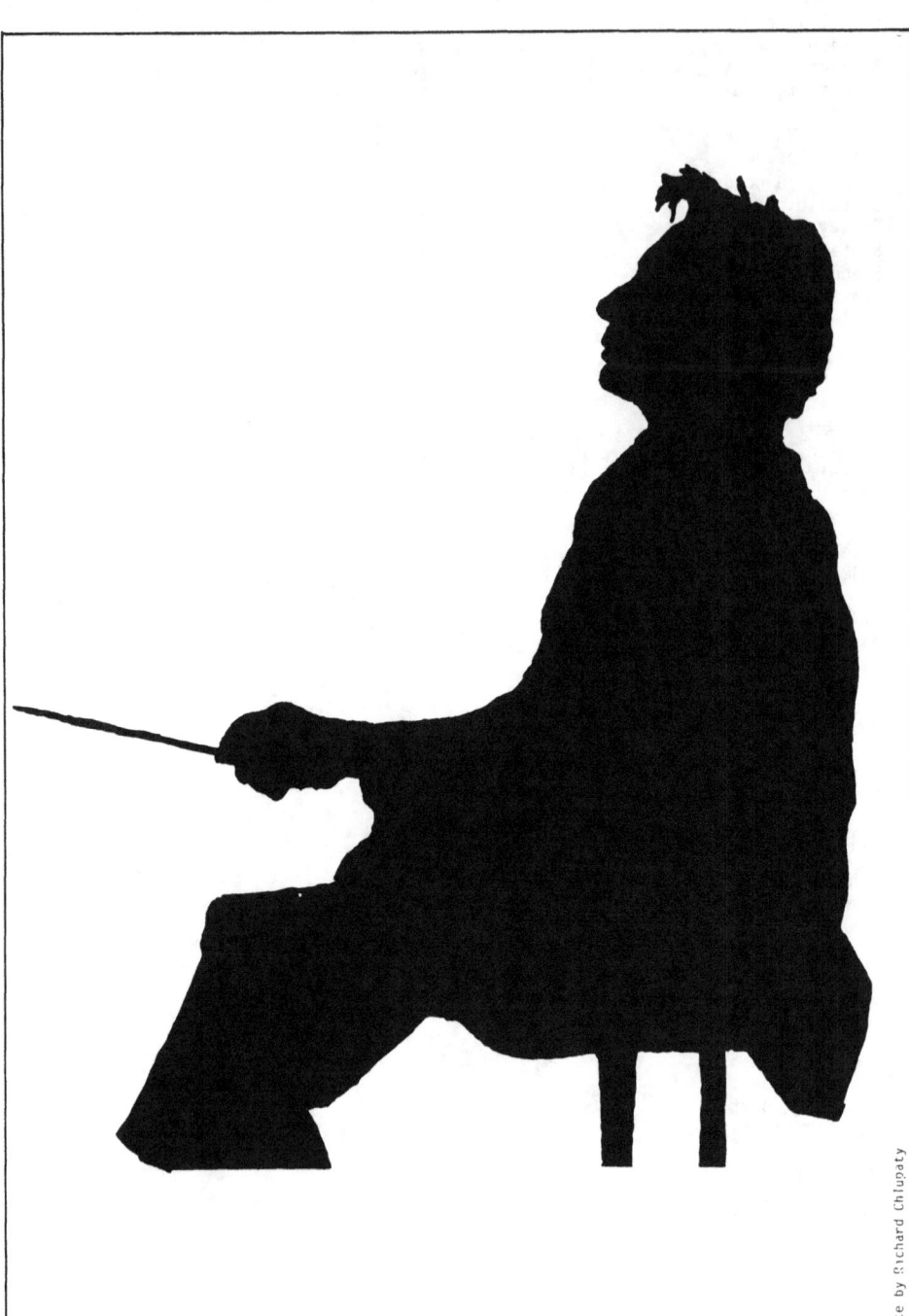

Silhouette by Richard Chlupaty

The video market for Western classical music is already well developed in Japan

Appendix B:
List of video recordings compiled by David Lampon

Information given is the participating orchestra, the year of production and names of the producer and film or TV company involved. Abbreviations:
ORF - Austrian Radio & TV;
ZDF - German TV Channel 2;
RAI - Italian Radio & TV

Strauss Der Rosenkavalier
VPO 1960 Czinner

Puccini La Bohème
La Scala 1965 Zeffirelli-Cosmotel

Schumann Symphony No 4
Vienna Symphony 1966
Clouzot-Cosmotel

Mozart Violin Concerto 5
Vienna Symphony/Menuhin
1966 Clouzot-Cosmotel

Dvorak Symphony No 9
BPO 1966 Clouzot-Cosmotel

Beethoven Symphony No 5
BPO 1966 Clouzot-Cosmotel

Bizet Carmen
VPO 1967 Karajan-Cosmotel

Bach Brandenburg Concerto No 3
BPO 1967 Reichenbach-Cosmotel

Bach Suite No 3
BPO 1967 Reichenbach-Cosmotel

Mozart Coronation Mass
RAI Rome 1967 Clouzot-Cosmotel

Wagner Die Walküre
(Rehearsal extract)
BPO 1967 Reichenbach-BBC

Verdi Requiem
La Scala 1967 Clouzot-Cosmotel

Mozart Divertimento No 17
BPO 1967

Brahms Symphony No 3
BPO 1967

Tchaikovsky Piano Concerto No 1
BPO/Weissenberg 1967
Falck-Cosmotel
Re-made in 1973

Beethoven Symphony No 6
BPO 1968 Niebeling-Unitel

Mascagni Cavalleria Rusticana
La Scala 1968
Falck-Cosmotel

Leoncavallo I Pagliacci
La Scala 1968
Karajan-Cosmotel

Beethoven Symphony No 9
BPO 1970 Karajan-Unitel

Berlioz Symphonie Fantastique
Orchestre de Paris 1971
Benamon-Cosmotel

Mozart 3-Piano Concerto
Orchestre de Paris
Eschenbach/Frantz/Karajan
Karajan-Unitel

Beethoven Symphony No 1
BPO 1972 Arnbom-Unitel

Beethoven Symphony No 2
BPO 1972 Scholz-Unitel

Beethoven Symphony No 3
BPO 1972 Niebeling-Unitel

Beethoven Symphony No 5
BPO 1972 Karajan-Unitel

Brahms Symphony No 1
BPO 1972 Karajan-Unitel

Brahms Symphony No 2
BPO 1972 Karajan-Unitel

Brahms Symphony No 3
BPO 1973 Karajan-UNitel

Brahms Symphony No 4
BPO 1973 Karajan-Unitel

Beethoven Symphony No 4
BPO 1973 Karajan-Unitel

Beethoven Symphony No 7
BPO 1973 Niebeling-Unitel

Beethoven Symphony No 8
BPO 1973 Scholz-Unitel

Rachmaninov Piano Concerto No 2
BPO/Weissenberg 1973
Karajan-Unitel

Tchaikovsky Symphony No 4
BPO 1973 Wild-Unitel

Tchaikovsky Symphony No 5
BPO 1973 Wild-Unitel

Tchaikovsky Symphony No 6
BPO 1974 Wild-Unitel

Verdi Otello
BPO 1974 Karajan-Unitel

Puccini Madama Butterfly
VPO 1974/5
Ponnelle-Unitel

Strauss Don Quixote
BPO/Rostropovich 1975
Karajan-Unitel

Beethoven Coriolan Overture
BPO 1975 Karajan-Unitel

Beethoven Egmont Overture
BPO 1975 Karajan-Unitel

Rossini William Tell
Overture
BPO 1975 Karajan-Unitel

Wagner Tannhäuser Overture
BPO 1975 Karajan Unitel

Weber Der Freischütz
Overture
BPO 1975 Karajan-Unitel

Wagner Die Meistersinger
Prelude
BPO 1975 Karajan-Unitel

Beethoven Symphony No 9
BPO 1977
Burton-ZDF-Unitel

Brahms Requiem
BPO 1978 Karajan-Unitel

Verdi Il Trovatore
VPO 1978 Karajan-Unitel

Debussy Prélude à l'après-
midi d'un faune
BPO 1978 Karajan-Unitel

Ravel Daphnis et Chloe
2nd Suite
BPO 1978 Karajan-Unitel

Bruckner Symphony No 9
VPO 1978 Karajan-Unitel

Bruckner Te Deum
VPO 1978 Karajan-Unitel

New Year's Eve Concert
Liszt/Suppé/Bizet/Mascagni
BPO 1978 Karajan-Unitel

Beethoven Missa Solemnis
BPO 1979 Karajan-Unitel

Bruckner Symphony No 8
VPO 1979 Karajan-Unitel

Wagner Das Rheingold
BPO 1980 Karajan-Unitel

Stravinsky Apollo
BPO 1980 Karajan-Unitel

Berlioz Symphonie
Fantastique
BPO 1980 Karajan-Unitel

Verdi Falstaff
VPO 1982 Karajan-ORF/ZDF

Beethoven Symphony No 3
BPO 1982 Karajan-ZDF

Beethoven Symphony No 5
BPO 1982
Karajan-Telemondial

Beethoven Symphony No 6
BPO 1982
Karajan-Telemondial

Strauss Der Rosenkavalier
VPO 1983 Karajan-ORF/ZDF

New Year's Eve Concert
Rossini/Smetana/Sibelius/
J.Strauss
BPO 1983 Karajan-ZDF

Strauss Alpine Symphony
BPO 1983 Karajan-ZDF

Brahms Requiem
VPO 1983
Karajan-Telemondial

Beethoven Symphony No 4
BPO 1983
Karajan-Telemondial

Beethoven Symphony No 7
BPO 1983
Karajan-Telemondial

Beethoven Symphony No 9
BPO 1983
Karajan-Telemondial

Beethoven Symphony No 8
BPO 1984
Karajan-Telemondial

Beethoven Symphony No 3
BPO 1984
Karajan-Telemondial

Beethoven Symphony No 1
BPO 1984
Karajan-Telemondial

Beethoven Symphony No 2
BPO 1984
Karajan-Telemondial

Strauss Metamorphosen and
Tod und Verklärung
BPO 1984 Karajan-ZDF

Strauss Ein Heldenleben
BPO 1984
Karajan-Telemondial

Verdi Requiem
VPO 1984
Karajan-Telemondial

Bruckner Te Deum
VPO 1984
Karajan-Telemondial

Tchaikovsky Symphony No 4
VPO 1984
Karajan-Telemondial

Tchaikovsky Symphony No 5
VPO 1984
Karajan-Telemondial

Tchaikovsky Symphony No 6
VPO 1984
Karajan-Telemondial

New Year's Eve Concert
Bach Violin Concerto/
Magnificat
BPO/Mutter 1984
Karajan-ZDF

Bruckner Symphony No 9
BPO 1985 Karajan-ZDF

Beethoven Egmont Overture
BPO 1985
Karajan-Telemondial

Beethoven Coriolan
Overture
BPO 1985
Karajan-Telemondial

Beethoven Fidelio Overture
BPO 1985
Karajan-Telemondial

Beethoven Leonore No 3
Overture
BPO 1985
Karajan-Telemondial

Dvorak Symphony No 8
VPO 1985
Karajan-Telemondial

Dvorak Symphony No 9
VPO 1985
Karajan-Telemondial

Smetana The Moldau
VPO 1985
Karajan-Telemondial

Strauss 4 Last Songs and
Closing Scene "Capriccio"
BPO/Tomowa-Sintow 1985
Karajan-Telemondial

Mozart Coronation Mass
VPO 1985
RAI-Polivideo

Beethoven Missa Solemnis
BPO 1985
Karajan-Telemondial

New Year's Eve Concert
Weber/Leoncavallo/Puccini
Liszt/Ravel/J.Strauss
BPO 1985 Burton-ZDF

Debussy La Mer
BPO 1985/6
Karajan-Telemondial

Debussy Prélude à l'après-
midi d'un faune
BPO 1985/6
Karajan-Telemondial

Ravel Pavane
BPO 1985/6
Karajan-Telemondial

Ravel Daphnis et Chloé,
2nd Suite
BPO 1985/6
Karajan-Telemondial

Mozart Requiem
VPO 1986
Karajan-Telemondial

Mussorgsky Pictures
BPO 1986
Karajan-Telemondial

Beethoven Symphony No 9
BPO 1986 Karajan-ZDF

Verdi Don Carlo
BPO 1986 Karajan-ORF/ZDF

Strauss Don Quixote
BPO 1986
Karajan-Telemondial

Ravel Bolero
BPO 1985
Karajan-Telemondial

Brahms The 4 Symphonies
BPO 1986/7
Karajan-Telemondial

New Year Concert
Strauss family
VPO 1987
Burton-ORF/ZDF-Telemondial

Ravel Rapsodie espagnole
BPO 1987
Karajan-Telemondial

Mozart Symphony No 29
BPO 1987
Karajan-Telemondial

Mozart Divertimento No 17
BPO 1987
Karajan-ZDF

Strauss Also sprach
Zarathustra
BPO 1987
Karajan-ZDF

Mozart Don Giovanni
VPO 1987
Hampe-ORF/ZDF

Appendix C:
A personal Top Twenty-five

The choices are listed alphabetically by composer. Appreciating that many LP collectors have not converted to CD, I am able to cheat and in many instances make separate recommendations for each category of listener. The number of highly recommended recordings therefore rises to 33 !

Beethoven   **Symphony No 6 "Pastoral"**

LP: Philharmonia/1953
Columbia 33CX 1124 or Toshiba EAC 37001-19
None of the later mock stereo versions acceptable (World Records, Electrola or EMI)

CD: BPO/1982
DG 413 932-2

Beethoven   **Symphony No 9 "Choral"**

LP and CD: BPO/1976
DG 415 832-1 and 415 832-2

Brahms   **Symphony No 2**

LP: Philharmonia/1955
EMI SXLP 30513
This vintage Philharmonia recording was given a new lease of life in the early 1980s by being issued in stereo for the first time

Bruckner   **Symphony No 8**

LP: BPO/1957
EMI CFP 41 4434-3

Bruckner   **Symphony No 7**

LP and CD: BPO/1975
DG 2707 102 and 419 195-2

Holst   **The Planets**

LP and CD: VPO/1961
Decca JB 30 and 417 709-2

Humperdinck	**Hänsel und Gretel**

LP: Philharmonia/1953
Columbia 33CX 1096/7 or EMI SLS 5145
EMI's stereo reprocessing on SLS 5145 only slightly disfigured the luxuriant sound of the mono original. Some years ago a German retail chain issued a limited edition of the recording in pure mono. This is my all-time favourite as an opera recording, and shows Karajan and the Philharmonia at the height of their powers together.

Liszt	**Orchestral Works**

LP and CD: BPO/various dates
DG 415 628-1 and 415 967-2

Mahler	**Symphony No 9**

CD only: BPO/1982
DG 410 726-2

Mozart	**Don Giovanni**

LP and CD: BPO/1985
DG 419 179-1 and 419 179-2
Most recent of a remarkable cycle of Mozart opera recordings by Karajan, a cycle which started with those made in Vienna in 1950. Listen here to the arias of Anna and Ottavio (two apiece), in which time stands still and we enter into the heart and mind of Giovanni's victims; this is achieved in no small measure by Karajan's accompaniment

Mozart	**Violin Concertos Nos 3 and 5**

LP and CD: BPO/Mutter 1977
DG 410 982-1 and 415 327-2

Mozart	**Requiem**

LP: BPO/1961
DG 2535 257

CD: VPO/1986
DG 419 610-2

Puccini	**Tosca**

LP: VPO/1962
Decca 5BB 132/4

CD: BPO/1979
DG 413 815-2

Sibelius	**Symphonies 4, 5 and 6**

LP: Symphonies 4 and 5   BPO/1976
EMI EG 29 06131

CD: Symphonies 4 and 6   BPO/1965 and 1967
DG 415 108-2

Strauss   Salome

   LP and CD: VPO/1977
   EMI SLS 5139 and CDS 749 3588

Strauss   Another opera

   LP: Ariadne auf Naxos Philharmonia/1954
   EMI RLS 760

   CD: Der Rosenkavalier Philharmonia/1956
   EMI CDS 749 3548

   It is difficult to choose between these two,
   but an interesting fact connects them:
   the roles of Composer and Zerbinetta in
   "Ariadne auf Naxos" are taken by the singers
   (Seefried and Streich) who were originally
   proposed to assume the parts of Octavian and
   Sophie in "Der Rosenkavalier" two years later;
   however, they were not available to take part
   when the time came, recording their parts
   later for Böhm and Deutsche Grammophon

Strauss   Ein Heldenleben

   LP and CD: BPO/1986
   DG 415 508-1 and 415 508-2

Strauss   Also sprach Zarathustra

   LP: BPO/1973
   DG 415 853-1

   CD: VPO/1959
   Decca 417 720-2

Verdi   Requiem Mass

   LP: VPO/1949
   Rodolphe RP 12403/4 or Discocorp RR 361

Verdi   Falstaff

   LP: Philharmonia/1956
   EMI SLS 5211

   CD: VPO/1980
   Philips 412 263-2

Verdi   Another opera

   LP: Don Carlo BPO/1978
   EMI SLS 5154

   CD: Il Trovatore VPO/1962
   Rodolphe RPC 32482/3 or Movimento Musica 012.001

Tchaikovsky	<u>Symphony No 6 "Pathétique"</u>

LP: VPO/1948 and 1949
Columbia 33CX 1026 or Toshiba EAC 30105

Wagner	<u>Parsifal</u>

LP and CD: BPO/1979 and 1980
DG 2741 002 and 413 347-2

Various composers	<u>Philharmonia Promenade Concert</u>

LP: Philharmonia/1960
EMI CFP 40368 or even better, if you can find it, the <u>mono</u> version on Columbia 33CX 1758 ! Like the producer of the LP, the late Walter Legge, I can often detect a more homogeneous blend of sound in Columbia mono records, even though a stereo version may have been produced at the same time

Various composers	<u>Albinoni Adagio; Pachelbel Canon; and others</u>

LP and CD: BPO/1983
DG 413 309-1 and 413 309-2
Baroque music played with "heart", not with "original instruments" ! Particularly delectable are the Mozart Serenata Notturna and Gluck Dance of the Blessed Spirits contained in this collection

Music and Books published by Travis & Emery Music Bookshop:

Anon.: Hymnarium Sarisburense, cum Rubris et Notis Musicus
Agricola, Johann Friedrich from Tosi: Anleitung zur Singkunst. (Faksimile 1757)
Bach, C.P.E.: edited W. Emery: Nekrolog or Obituary Notice of J.S. Bach.
Bateson, Naomi Judith: Alcock of Salisbury
Bathe, William: A Briefe Introduction to the Skill of Song
Bax, Arnold: Symphony #5, Arranged for Piano Four Hands by Walter Emery
Burney, Charles: The Present State of Music in France and Italy
Burney, Charles: The Present State of Music in Germany, The Netherlands …
Burney, Charles: An Account of the Musical Performances … Handel
Burney, Karl: Nachricht von Georg Friedrich Handel's Lebensumstanden.
Cobbett, W.W.: Cobbett's Cyclopedic Survey of Chamber Music. (2 vols.)
Corrette, Michel: Le Maitre de Clavecin
Crimp, Bryan: Dear Mr. Rosenthal … Dear Mr. Gaisberg …
Crimp, Bryan: Solo: The Biography of Solomon
d'Indy, Vincent: Beethoven: Biographie Critique
d'Indy, Vincent: Beethoven: A Critical Biography
d'Indy, Vincent: César Franck (in French)
Frescobaldi, Girolamo: D'Arie Musicali per Cantarsi. Primo Libro & Secondo Libro.
Geminiani, Francesco: The Art of Playing the Violin.
Handel; Purcell; Boyce; Geene et al: Calliope or English Harmony: Volume First.
Hawkins, John: A General History of the Science and Practice of Music (5 vols.)
Herbert-Caesari, Edgar: The Science and Sensations of Vocal Tone
Herbert-Caesari, Edgar: Vocal Truth
Hopkins and Rimboult: The Organ. Its History and Construction.
Hunt, John: Adam to Webern: the recordings of von Karajan
Isaacs, Lewis: Hänsel and Gretel. A Guide to Humperdinck's Opera.
Isaacs, Lewis: Königskinder (Royal Children) A Guide to Humperdinck's Opera.
Lacassagne, M. l'Abbé Joseph : Traité Général des élémens du Chant.
Lascelles (née Catley), Anne: The Life of Miss Anne Catley.
Mainwaring, John: Memoirs of the Life of the Late George Frederic Handel
Malcolm, Alexander: A Treaty of Music: Speculative, Practical and Historical
Marx, Adolph Bernhard: Die Kunst des Gesanges, Theoretisch-Practisch
May, Florence: The Life of Brahms
Mellers, Wilfrid: Angels of the Night: Popular Female Singers of Our Time
Mellers, Wilfrid: Bach and the Dance of God
Mellers, Wilfrid: Beethoven and the Voice of God
Mellers, Wilfrid: Caliban Reborn - Renewal in Twentieth Century Music
Mellers, Wilfrid: François Couperin and the French Classical Tradition

Travis & Emery Music Bookshop
17 Cecil Court, London, WC2N 4EZ, United Kingdom.
Tel. (+44) 20 7240 2129

Music and Books published by Travis & Emery Music Bookshop:

Mellers, Wilfrid: Harmonious Meeting
Mellers, Wilfrid: Le Jardin Retrouvé, The Music of Frederic Mompou
Mellers, Wilfrid: Music and Society, England and the European Tradition
Mellers, Wilfrid: Music in a New Found Land: ... ... American Music
Mellers, Wilfrid: Romanticism and the Twentieth Century (from 1800)
Mellers, Wilfrid: The Masks of Orpheus: …… the Story of European Music.
Mellers, Wilfrid: The Sonata Principle (from c. 1750)
Mellers, Wilfrid: Vaughan Williams and the Vision of Albion
Panchianio, Cattuffio: Rutzvanscad Il Giovine
Pearce, Charles: Sims Reeves, Fifty Years of Music in England.
Pettitt, Stephen: Philharmonia Orchestra: complete discography
Playford, John: An Introduction to the Skill of Musick.
Purcell, Henry et al: Harmonia Sacra ... The First Book, (1726)
Purcell, Henry et al: Harmonia Sacra ... Book II (1726)
Quantz, Johann: Versuch einer Anweisung die Flöte traversiere zu spielen.
Rameau, Jean-Philippe: Code de Musique Pratique, ou Methodes.
Rastall, Richard: The Notation of Western Music.
Rimbault, Edward: The Pianoforte, Its Origins, Progress, and Construction.
Rousseau, Jean Jacques: Dictionnaire de Musique
Rubinstein, Anton : Guide to the proper use of the Pianoforte Pedals.
Sainsbury, John S.: Dictionary of Musicians. Vol. 1. (1825). 2 vols.
Simpson, Christopher: A Compendium of Practical Musick in Five Parts
Spohr, Louis: Autobiography
Spohr, Louis: Grand Violin School
Tans'ur, William: A New Musical Grammar; or The Harmonical Spectator
Terry, Charles Sanford: Four-Part Chorals of J.S. Bach. (German & English)
Terry, Charles Sanford: Joh. Seb. Bach, Cantata Texts, Sacred and Secular.
Terry, Charles Sanford: The Origins of the Family of Bach Musicians.
Tosi, Pierfrancesco: Opinioni de' Cantori Antichi, e Moderni
Van der Straeten, Edmund: History of the Violoncello, The Viol da Gamba ...
Van der Straeten, Edmund: History of the Violin, Its Ancestors... (2 vols.)
Walther, J. G.: Musicalisches Lexikon ober Musicalische Bibliothec (1732)

Travis & Emery Music Bookshop
17 Cecil Court, London, WC2N 4EZ, United Kingdom.
Tel. (+44) 20 7240 2129

© Travis & Emery 2009

www.ingramcontent.com/pod-product-compliance
Lightning Source LLC
Chambersburg PA
CBHW071850230426
43671CB00012B/2130